SUCCEEDING AS AN INDU

D1644332

SUCCEEDING AS AN INDUCTION TUTOR

Clive Carroll
Neil Simco

Learning Matters

First published in 2001 by Learning Matters Ltd.

British Library Cataloguing in Publication Data
A CIP record for this book is available from the British Library.

ISBN 1 903300 23 1

Cover design by Topics – The Creative Partnership
Project management by Deer Park Productions
Typeset and illustrated by PDQ Typesetting
Printed and bound in Great Britain by Bell & Bain Ltd., Glasgow

Learning Matters Ltd
58 Wonford Road
Exeter EX2 4LQ
Tel: 01392 215560
Email: info@learningmatters.co.uk
www.learningmatters.co.uk

CONTENTS

For us, *Succeeding as an Induction Tutor* has been an important book to write. The induction tutor has a fundamentally important role to play in early professional development. There are major issues in the profession about recruitment and retention, and it is interesting to note there is some emerging evidence that good-quality professional development opportunities correlate closely with retaining young/beginning teachers in the profession. In the USA, the Connecticut State Department has invested heavily in a programme for new teachers (over a period of three years). It is interesting to note the retention rate in that state is very much above the national average and, whilst it is simplistic to say this is down to induction alone, it seems appropriate to suggest that good-quality professional development is a major factor in ensuring teachers stay with teaching. If you feel valued and supported you are less likely to seek alternative employment. We do hope you are able to share this vision with us.

To this end, we have developed accredited training and support for induction tutors that we deliver nationally. The emphasis is on practical, useful approaches that mirror good classroom and management practice. The format of the training is as follows:

Summary of the content of a three-day course for induction tutors

Day 1 – getting started

- **What is good practice?**
- **The roles and responsibilities of those involved.**
- **Reviewing the current situation in your school.**
- **The current statutory DfEE requirements and TTA guidance.**
- **Producing a draft policy.**
- **The Career Entry Profile (CEP).**

Day 2 – developing the skills

- **Learning and teaching – using the Qualified Teacher Status (QTS) standards.**
- **Managing the process of classroom observation and review.**
- **Links with performance management.**

Day 3 – moving on

- **Reflection and review of the experience following Day 2.**
- **Monitoring progress.**
- **Managing review and assessment objectives.**
- **The process of setting and achieving objectives.**
- **Guidance on accredited work.**

For further information on this training, please contact the authors at the Education Development Unit, St Martin's College – tel: 015394 30250.

Acknowledgements

In writing this book, we would like to acknowledge a number of sources. We place enormous value on the experience of our work with several hundred induction tutors who have contributed to our thinking on courses during recent years. In addition, we have appreciated teachers' input into the case studies and illustrations. They gave freely of their time and energy. No real names have been used to avoid identification of teachers – we can only go so far as identifying areas of the country from which they come. These are Birmingham, Cumbria and the east of Yorkshire. We can, however, mention administrative support that has been crucial in developing the manuscript and painstakingly accommodating our frequent additions, amendments, etc. In all this, Paula Mitchell and Susan Cockburn have provided outstanding service. Clive would like to thank Paul Ginnis for his insightful suggestions on classroom practice and Peter Batty and Vanessa Champion at the Education Development Unit, St Martin's College, for their influence on thinking and practice with regard to interpersonal skills development. Acknowledgement is also given to the Teacher Training Agency (TTA). Neil was involved in the development of national support materials in 1999, and some of the work of the small group he led has been used to underpin Chapters 3 and 4, although it is recast in a very different form. We would also like to acknowledge the work of Jill Staley and John Carr at the TTA who have been the architects of the national induction year arrangements, creating a workable system within the framework provided by government ministers. The DfEE has given permission for reproducing the national pro formas in Chapter 4. Finally, we would like to acknowledge our families' understanding that preparing a book takes time. Preparing this book has, on occasion, prevented us from being able to take advantage of all our leisure time! We therefore feel it right and proper to dedicate this book to our respective daughters, Amy and Beth.

Clive Carroll and Neil Simco

In September 1999, new arrangements for the induction of newly qualified teachers (NQTs) came into operation in England (DfEE, 1999). These new arrangements are highly significant because, for the first time, a national system for induction has been created that centres on the twin pillars of assessment and entitlement. NQTs are assessed against a range of nationally defined standards. The assessment is recorded on nationally defined pro formas, and there is a national system to deal with any failures to meet the induction period requirements. Likewise, NQTs have explicit entitlement to a 90% timetable (compared to that of other teachers in the school), have access to a properly planned programme of professional development (based on the specification of 'individually tailored' professional objectives) and are to be observed teaching at regular intervals.

Taken together, we would argue that the new arrangements raise the stakes in induction. Many NQTs now have clear expectations about the elements of their entitlement and an enhanced expectation about the nature of their professional development within the induction period. They are also clear that, should they fail to meet the induction period requirements then, subject to the appeals process taking its course, they will be barred from teaching in state schools. For induction tutors, too, the stakes are raised. There are enhanced and very clear professional benefits in relation to developing or acquiring the skills of observing, discussing and assessing practice. These are readily transferable to other contexts (particularly working within initial teacher training and performance management) and it is also the case that mentoring is becoming a core professional skill rather than an option some choose to follow. Yet the role of induction tutor is a responsible role. You would have some responsibility for ensuring your NQT has clearly focused opportunities for professional development in relation to a range of specified targets, for assessing your NQT against those targets and, thereby, allowing the NQT to become a fully fledged professional. In essence the role of the induction tutor is to act as gatekeeper to the teaching profession. This carries with it authority. It also carries responsibility.

The purpose of this book is to provide you, as induction tutor, with clear practical advice to support your work with NQTs. *Succeeding as an Induction Tutor* is the parallel volume to *Succeeding in the Induction Year* (also published by Learning Matters and directed to NQTs – Simco, 2000). In this book you will find a mixture of suggestions for developing effective practice, case studies and commentaries, together with a large number of illustrations related to the induction year. The book covers the whole of the primary and secondary age ranges (including special education), with material being drawn from NQTs in a wide range of schools. You will not find we have 'done the job' for you as we want to encourage you to engage with the ideas for practice contained within this book. For example, we have not provided you with an example of a school policy but have provided a detailed framework to help you prepare one for yourself. There needs to be a recognition about the uniqueness of every induction tutor situation, from the two-teacher rural primary school to the large urban city technology college. Indeed, we would argue that the most effective induction tutoring of all is one that understands the national framework but that is able to apply this very clearly to the individual circumstances of the school.

It is not our intention you should read the book from cover to cover. Rather like *Succeeding in the Induction Year*, it is suggested you may wish to use this as a resource and, in this way, you will wish to dip in an out of it as you address particular issues that might arise from time to time in your induction tutoring. Notwithstanding this, we would like to mention there are a number of common strands that run through the book. Each of these reflects our approach to induction, and we hope you well feel able to engage with us about these perspectives.

In the first place, we would like to reiterate the point made above. This book is practical and focused on acting to support the development of your work with your NQTs. It is, however, done *with* you, not *to* you. Examples are used to illustrate points of principle, but these are not necessarily panaceas for good practice; rather, they are illustrations within particular contexts. It follows that the detail of effective induction practice in one school may not be effective at all in another.

In the second instance, we believe that succeeding as an effective induction tutor involves more than complying with a set of national arrangements. The advantage of these is they provide a detailed central framework. The disadvantage is that they can reduce the role of the induction tutor to a list of 'jobs to do'. As you read the book you will see that the generic notions of effective learning and teaching provide a backcloth for the idea of effective induction tutoring. The effective induction tutor is someone who not only knows intuitively what constitutes effective teaching but who is also in a position to make this quite explicit in professional conversation. It also implies the effective induction tutor is curious about teaching and learning. Even when the freedom to make decisions about pedagogy and curriculum content is more constrained than used to be the case, the induction tutor is able to see alternative ways forward that are responsive to the learning occurring within the classroom.

All this links to the three Dewey (1933) maxims of open-mindedness, whole-heartedness and responsibility. These are as true now as they were in 1933 and can be applied to a multitude of educational settings. Open-mindedness involves the desire to listen to many different perspectives before coming to decisions. The effective induction tutor will gather evidence from a multitude of sources prior to making decisions about the assessment of the NQT. Whole-heartedness is concerned with passion and commitment. At a recent event for induction tutors, one was heard to say she was fairly single-minded in ensuring her NQT had a productive experience because this was very different from that which she experienced as a probationary teacher some years previously. Finally comes responsibility – that the role of the induction tutor carries with it professional responsibility as well as authority. None of us will forget those first weeks and month as teachers!

A third strand that runs through the book has already been mentioned in passing. This is the idea that mentoring is rapidly becoming a core professional skill rather than something that is within the role description of a small number of specialised teachers. Mentoring has application within initial teacher training, performance management and induction. Some primary schools are now in a position where every member of staff is trained as a mentor and practises this in a wide range of contexts. It is interesting to note the DfEE *Code of Practice for Providers of Professional Development for Teachers* (2001), which suggests that the notion of schools as professional learning communities will be increasingly important. It is arguably almost impossible to achieve this outside a mentoring culture. The same document outlines a range of national priorities for continuing professional development, one of which is training to enhance teachers' core mentoring skills so these can be applied in a variety of ways.

These three strands can be seen in the various chapters of this book. Chapter 1 is focused on the key roles and responsibilities of the induction tutor. It may be of particular interest if you are starting off as an induction tutor as it will help you to anticipate what is involved. This chapter is careful to draw a distinction between the idea of role and that of responsibility, because too often elements of teachers' work are reduced to a mere job description. These are important, of course, but the idea of role is equally so because it defines the overall professional area that underpins, in this case, effective induction tutoring. You will also find in this chapter an honest analysis of the professional benefits and costs associated with this role.

Chapter 2 builds on Chapter 1 in as much as it considers approaches to preparing for effective induction. We are particularly keen to suggest that an essential part of preparing to be an induction tutor is concerned with understanding notions of teaching and learning, and being able to verbalise these effectively. This underpins our idea that the success one has as an induction tutor is not related to the quality of the 'training' that is 'delivered'; rather, it is derived from the deep understanding of teaching and learning processes you will have acquired over the time you have been in teaching. In one sense effective induction tutoring relates to a bringing to the forefront of consciousness all the professional actions and strategies you use every day of your working life. The chapter addresses these fairly deeply rooted ideas and also explores practical tasks that need to occur, such as writing or updating your school policy on induction – and it goes without saying we see this particular activity as a catalyst for change, not a paper exercise!

Chapters 3 and 4 are closely linked and really form the central core of the book. Taken together, they represent the twin pillars underpinning the induction year – on the one hand monitoring and support and, on the other, assessment. You may wish to read them in conjunction with the parallel chapters in *Succeeding in the Induction Year*. Monitoring and support cover key areas, such as the use of the Career Entry Profile, the running of effective meetings, approaches to observation and the creation of individual development plans. These areas are amply illustrated with case-study material and we hope you will find the material directly relevant to your work as an induction tutor.

Chapter 4 focuses on the assessment of the induction year. It attempts to suggest a strategy for making the national requirements as manageable as possible whilst retaining rigour and validity in assessment. The chapter provides practical advice on the nature of the assessment meetings, on writing report pro formas, on strategies for involving the NQT in the process and the appropriate use of the standards to underpin the entire process. In particular, the chapter considers the role of evidence in the assessment process and identifies a range of key strategies for dealing with the very small number of NQTs who may be at risk of not meeting the requirements for induction.

Throughout the book, there are a number of chapters that include illustrations and case studies that have been taken from empirical work we have done in preparation for this book. The final chapter focuses very much on mini case studies where we tell the story of five teachers' experience of the induction period. In a sense this is a coming together of the major strands that describe the essence of the book. In these case studies we simply tell the story of the experience of the induction year as told by the induction tutors. Our aim here is to provide a worthwhile and vivid account of five real situations to give you encouragement and food for thought. Following each account we have prepared a brief commentary and some points to ponder. We hope you will value engaging with these as they will enable you to respond to some of the *major* themes of the book.

In this chapter you will find material that will help you to:

- **understand the nature of your role as induction tutor;**
- **appreciate the key responsibilities associated with this role;**
- **understand the relationship between induction tutoring and the 'big picture' of mentoring, including performance management and mentoring in initial teacher training;**
- **identify the key professional benefits of induction tutoring;**
- **clarify possible costs in terms of commitment and time.**

Introduction and chapter overview

We would argue that a key part of any professional activity is to be clear about both the role and the responsibilities associated with this activity. This is no less true of induction and is, perhaps, particularly important for at least two reasons. The first is that we all carry around in our minds images associated with the support and monitoring we received when we were probationary teachers or newly qualified teachers (NQTs), and it will also be true that, in many cases, these images would not be in line with the intentions of the national framework for induction. It is almost certainly the case that, if we could have an instant insight into all the readers of this book, the variety of this experience would be enormous. One of the key changes since the current national arrangements were introduced is that there is an aim of ensuring the monitoring and support provided to NQTs are broadly consistent within and between schools and are focused on an individual professional development plan. It may be as well to dispel our experiences as new teachers and to focus on the current intentions, purposes and procedures of induction. A second reason why it is important to be clear about roles and responsibilities is because of the significance of the role. Whilst it is not true to say that an NQT's experience stands or falls on the quality of the induction tutoring it is, however, true to say this is a significant factor. As induction tutor you are in a powerful position, and your tutoring will have a real impact on your NQT's development, or lack of it. It is particularly important you accept your responsibility to ensure your NQT is aware of his or her responsibilities within the year. The significance of your role is seen in this comment from an NQT:

> I feel valued and respected. I know what is expected of me and recognise what I do well. My progress is clear to me and is recognised by others. I can see where I need to improve and I am working, with help, on some strategies to help me achieve my goals. Yes it is tough and challenging, but the quality of professional opportunity for me to move forward here is excellent. Yes, my dream is intact.

In order to address some of these issues, this chapter is divided into four sections, each of which considers a different aspect of the role of the induction tutor. Section I focuses on the role of the induction tutor. Here we distinguish between the notion of 'role' and the responsibilities that exist within this.

In section 2 there is a fuller consideration of the responsibilities of the induction tutor. This section interprets the national framework for induction and provides you with an overview of the key responsibilities and how these relate to you as induction tutor. It also shows how your responsibilities relate to those held by others.

Section 3 considers the 'big picture' in mentoring. Here there is a suggestion that mentoring is no longer an optional extra for some teachers who choose to take a particular career path but is actually a core professional skill. We show how the roles and responsibilities associated with induction tutoring relate to those that are apparent in both initial teacher training (ITT) and performance management. Your work as induction tutor will clearly take place within a much wider professional context.

Section 4 focuses on the key professional benefits of induction tutoring for you as induction tutor and for others associated with this role. It also seeks to identify, honestly, some of the costs involved!

Section One

The role of the induction tutor

'Induction tutor' is, in brief, a term used to describe the mentor who has responsibility for work with NQTs in a variety of ways. In practice, this person will work in very different ways according to context. Many large secondary schools will have a continuing professional development co-ordinator who heads a team of induction tutors with clear distinctions being made between the monitoring and assessing roles. In a small primary school, the induction tutor might also be the headteacher and, here, the school may wish to deploy another colleague to support the assessment role or may request LEA inspector/adviser support within the assessment process.

Whatever the context, in our view, a careful distinction needs to be made between the notion of role and that of responsibility. Role is concerned with different aspects of the professional activity that is associated with teaching. In this way the induction tutor will sometimes be a facilitator; at other times, an assessor. It may be useful in this respect to consider that the induction tutor has a number of 'roles' as leader, manager, etc., and we consider this in more detail below. The word 'for' is significant in arriving at a definition of responsibilities because, as induction tutor, you will have responsibilities towards a range of people, towards yourself, your NQTs, your headteacher and so forth. It is in the dynamic between roles and responsibilities that the actual job description of the induction tutor can be defined, as we shall see below.

In our view the induction tutor has six key roles:

1. *Teacher role*. This needs to be at the top of the list because your professional

practice will be very public to your NQT. The role involves understanding teaching and learning and being able both to model this and to articulate an informed view of what quality means in teaching and learning. It involves knowing about current initiatives in curriculum development and in teaching styles and strategies.

2. *Facilitator role*. A key part of the role of the induction tutor is to facilitate the professional development of the NQT. First, this will involve diagnosing the needs of the NQT In close collaboration with him or her and through using the Career Entry Profile (CEP). Secondly, it will use this analysis to work with the NQT to design an individual development plan such that the NQT can observe, be observed, attend relevant courses and have opportunities for professional dialogue. This is perhaps the essence of the role of the induction tutor.

3. *Leader role*. As induction tutor, you will have a role to provide leadership to the whole process of induction. This will mean you will need to understand the national framework, be able to apply this into school policy and be proactive in setting up meetings with your NQT.

4. *Manager/co-ordinator role*. Linked to the leader role, this element will involve you as induction tutor liaising with others to ensure the purposes and processes of the induction year are met and fulfilled. A particular element of this role will be to ensure a measure of consistency is apparent, particularly if you have more than one NQT in school.

5. *Assessor role*. The assessor role is the one that is particularly emphasised within the new arrangements for induction. This is explored in depth in Chapter 4, but the role centres on you being involved in making judgements about whether the NQT has met the standard national requirements of the induction year. There is clearly a summative element here but, throughout the year, there is also a formative element in regard to diagnosing the NQT's professional development needs.

6. *Sponsor and representative role*. A final part of the role is to act, from time to time, as advocate for the NQT. This may involve such activities as ensuring the NQT has access to a range of INSET opportunities and making sure all colleagues in school ensure the entitlement the NQT has is properly understood.

Yeomans and Sampson (1995) have analysed the role of mentor. As you can see, there are three key elements here. The first is structural where the mentor sets out the framework for, in this case, the induction period. The second is the supportive role and the third is what Yeomans and Sampson term the 'professional' element. We would argue that a main implication of the current arrangements is a move away from a notion of the mentor as a host/friend/counsellor towards one where the professional elements have a much higher status. The central elements of the role are about ensuring entitlement is met and assessment is rigorous and fair. It is because of this distinction that, in some schools, an additional member of staff is allocated to the NQT who has a more informal role to act a confidant and friend. We believe this is a

Mentors – roles, strategies, skills and qualities	
Dimension	**Role**
Structural	Planner
	Organiser
	Negotiator
	Inductor
Supportive	Host
	Friend
	Counsellor
Professional	Trainer
	Educator
	Assessor

From Yeomans and Sampson (1995).

good strategy because it separates out the professional core from the wider issues NQTs may wish to talk about with others from time to time.

It is also significant that many aspects of the role involve skills, qualities and attributes that are also apparent in the roles of senior managers in schools and, indeed, in many cases, the role of the induction tutor is fulfilled by colleagues with an appropriate level of experience. This may be a deputy head or a teacher responsible for ITT students in a primary school, or the head of department in a secondary school. In many situations, in both primary and secondary schools, the induction tutor has substantial experience of working with ITT students because there is a great deal of common ground in the professional skills required for working in induction and in ITT. It is in this sense that mentoring is becoming a core professional skill that is desirable for all teachers but essential for those who have aspirations for senior management. The following example provides an account of the career path Gemma took:

Gemma began her teaching career in 1991 in a large junior school in a socially deprived area of a northern city. After her first year of teaching, she became involved in ITT with a local university. This was at the time when schools were beginning to take the lead responsibility for both supervising and assessing student teachers. She undertook a basic mentor-training course that explored such key areas as observation of students, conducting tutorials, assessing students' competence and the national framework for ITT. Two years later, Gemma undertook an advanced course in mentoring that led to a university qualification and, during this period, she broadened her experience by mentoring students in another school, mentoring NQTs and, additionally, she became involved in peer review and appraisal. All this experience was a significant strength when she applied for National Professional Qualification for Headteachers (NPQH) status: her mentoring experience was recognised as a key attribute. Currently in a deputy head's post in another school, Gemma is working closely alongside the head and using her mentoring expertise to introduce performance management processes into the school. Gemma recognised the significance of mentoring at a very early stage in her career and worked to develop this as a core professional skill.

The responsibilities of the induction tutor   Section Two

The key responsibilities of the induction tutor are identified clearly in Circular 0090/2000 (DfEE, 2000c), although few specific details are given. Paragraph 26 states:

> The induction tutor should be fully aware of the requirements of the induction period and should have the necessary skills, expertise and knowledge to work effectively in the role. In particular, the induction tutor should be able to make rigorous and fair judgements about the NQT's performance in relation to the requirements for satisfactory completion of the induction period and to provide or co-ordinate guidance and effective support for the NQT's professional development.

The responsibilities are related to a number of key areas:

- **First, as induction tutor, you should have a knowledge and skills base to equip you to fulfil the role. This implies the role does involve an obligation to acquire new professional skills or to develop existing ones further. You may already be aware that a range of courses for induction tutors have been established and run by LEAs and higher education institutions. We believe the first sentence in the quotation from the circular cited above is important because it gives a clear indication the induction tutor's role demands specific professional skills and that it is up to the prospective induction tutor to develop these.**

- **It is perhaps significant that, in the second sentence of the paragraph, the responsibilities related to assessment are mentioned first. This is the major new element in the current arrangements for induction. When the old probationary year was abandoned by the then Secretary of State for Education, Kenneth Clarke, the first version of the induction year did not contain any formal requirements for summative assessment, focusing instead on professional development. The current arrangements adopt an approach that, in many ways, is the exact opposite. There is a requirement for detailed but, we believe, manageable assessments to be made against national criteria.**

- **The third area of responsibility relates to ensuring the NQT has his or her entitlement and this involves elements such as the induction tutor devising an individual professional development plan, making arrangements for NQTs to observe in other classes and making arrangements so NQTs are able to attend INSET courses.**

Using these three areas, it is possible to prepare a job specification for the induction tutor that outlines in more detail the requirements of the role. We hope schools may wish to adapt this to their own particular circumstances.

As the primary audience for this book is the induction tutor, we have chosen to focus on the roles and responsibilities associated with induction tutoring. Figure I describes an induction tutor's activities and describes his or her responsibilities within the context of various roles (it will not escape your thinking that the knowledge and skills required to undertake this work transfer into may other aspects of the work of experienced teachers and promoted postholders, e.g. curriculum co-ordinators,

A job specification for induction tutors

1. Professional development responsibilities

The induction tutor should:

- Ensure an adequate knowledge base is acquired in relation to the national framework for induction that focuses on monitoring and support and assessment of the induction year.
- Ensure skills are refined or acquired in relation to monitoring, support, assessing professional practice and managing the work of others in relation to the NQT.
- Ensure he or she has an informed knowledge and understanding of what constitutes high quality in teaching and learning so that a model of good practice is provided for the NQT.

2. Assessing professional practice

The induction tutor should, in liaison with the headteacher or senior manager responsible for NQT induction:

- Understand the nature of the three assessment meetings in the induction year and be familiar with the standards for Qualified Teacher Status and the induction standards that underpin these.
- Be able to conduct these assessment meetings in a rigorous but fair manner, using a wide range of appropriate evidence and, in particular,
    - be able to make valid assessments based on observations of the NQT's teaching.
- Complete the national assessment pro formas following the meetings.
- Understand the importance of early diagnosis and intervention in the case of NQTs who are at risk of failing to meet the requirements of the induction period.

3. Providing effective monitoring and support

The induction tutor should:

- Review the NQT's Career Entry profile at the beginning of the induction year and ensure an individual professional development programme based on specified appropriate professional targets is developed.
- Create a professional relationship with the NQT that is characterised by openness, honesty and trust.
- Ensure the professional development programme is put into practice. This will involve elements such as facilitating the NQT to observe in other classes or schools, teaching collaboratively with the NQT, ensuring the NQT attends relevant INSET courses.
- Review the NQT's professional objectives at three professional review meetings, one in each term.
- Observe the NQT teaching at least once per half term.
- Review professional development objectives at the end of the induction year in preparation for the second year of teaching.
- Ensure the NQT is fully aware of his or her own responsibilities in the induction period in regard to his or her own professional development.
- Ensure a range of colleagues is actively involved in the mentoring process.
- In liaison with the headteacher, ensure the entitlement of an additional 10% non-contact time (10% of a normal timetable) is achieved.

Responsibilities for: / Roles as:	Yourself	Managing the induction and support of NQTs in the school	Being mentor on a 1:1 basis for one or more NQTS	Monitoring and assessment of (a) one new colleague and /or (b) all NQTs
Teacher	Keep up to date with current developments in teaching and learning.		• Engage in curriculum discussion about good practice. • Be observed when working with pupils.	
Facilitator	• Seek to develop your own skills, knowledge and understanding in these roles. • Seek opportunities to review your practice in these roles on your own and with others.	• Use the Career Entry Profile. • Develop a programme which relates to whole-school needs and the individual needs of the NQT.	• Arrange for NQT to observe good practice. • Work with him or her/observe him or her at work. • Create opportunities to discuss with precision.	• Arrange for NQT to be observed for assessment purposes and ensure the process is consistently managed.
Leader	• Identify those areas where you feel confident – develop and sustain these. • Identify those areas where you feel less confident and plan to develop them.	• Ensure there is a policy, programme and process based on shared and understood principles. • Provide in-school support for mentor.	• Provide leadership in the partnership (e.g. proactive/setting up of meetings).	• Ensure the assessment/monitoring part of the process is understood and assessors are clear about their role.
Manager/co-ordinator		• Manage the day-to-day arrangements. • Organise meetings to support development. • Provide documentation for SMT.	• Ensure the purposes of the induction year are reviewed regularly and met. • Ensure consistency in the management of the process of classroom observation, review and target-setting.	• Ensure monitoring and assessment is balanced – spread out over the term – documented useful to all parties.
Assessor		• Ensure colleagues understand requirements for assessment.	• Ensure all parties understand the process of monitoring and assessment.	• Observe and assess in classrooms. • Manage review and give feedback.
Sponsor and representative		• Provide sensitive information/guidance to staff.	• Ensure they have access to LEA INSET opportunities for NQTs.	• Ensure the process is properly understood and represent the NQT where there are misunderstandings.

Figure I. Induction tutor: roles and responsibilities for NQTs. This matrix is a tool to help you think through the implications of this work. It is in no way intended to be definitive.

subject leaders, heads of department and, indeed, senior managers). This is really a starting point for discussion. It may well be the case you could use this as a blank matrix for a starting point for staff discussion about roles and responsibilities in regard to the induction year. The exact nature of these will certainly vary across primary and secondary phases, but they will also vary within phases. However, it is clearly the case that induction tutoring does not take place in isolation. Of particular importance is the role of the headteacher, who has a clear function to create a context in which the three key areas of the induction tutor's responsibility can be fulfilled. The headteacher's responsibilities focus on ensuring the induction programme that is established is appropriate and that the assessment procedures are both fair and rigorous. We consider that the various roles the headteacher has in relation to induction can be expressed within the headteacher's various areas of responsibility. We also feel the headteacher has a critical role in supporting your work as an induction tutor. The professional benefits for you are clear, but so are the responsibilities – and it is important you have the permitting circumstances to carry out your role effectively.

Before we move on to the next section, we would like briefly to explore the responsibilities of the NQT throughout the induction year. It is clear to us that, while the role of the induction tutor and headteacher is substantial, it is not unlimited. The NQT is a qualified professional and that status carries with it real responsibility. In particular, the NQT has the responsibility to engage fully with the individual professional development plan you have set up. NQTs need to be proactive in suggesting appropriate activities to take their learning forward and need, from time to time, to organise (following discussion about professional objectives) visits to other schools and other relevant activities. Likewise, the NQT has a responsibility to ensure his or her CEP is made available to you at the beginning of the year. If NQTs feel the support they are receiving is inadequate, they have an obligation to make their views known. This would normally be within the school in the first instance, but could involve the LEA should a situation remain unresolved. As induction tutor you would have a responsibility to inform the NQT of the name of the relevant LEA officer for NQTs.

There will be a tiny minority of NQTs who are at risk of failing to meet the requirements of the induction year. This is always problematic, not only for the NQT but also for the induction tutor as the stakes are so high. Our view is that the clear definition of roles and responsibilities is absolutely essential in such cases. It is the responsibility of the induction tutor (working in close liaison with the headteacher) to diagnose the nature of the difficulty, to ensure the NQT knows he or she is at risk of failing to meet the induction year requirements and to put in place an action plan with clear measurable goals that can be assessed. Part of this responsibility is concerned with early intervention. To diagnose a difficulty well into the final term will almost certainly not leave enough time for the NQT to have a reasonable chance of addressing the problems. It is not the responsibility of the induction tutor actually to make the progress! This lies with the NQT, who has a duty to engage with the action plan. All this is important in any appeal situation. If the NQT is deemed not to have met the requirements of the induction period and subsequently appeals, the level of support offered will be scrutinised by the appeals panel. In particular, there would be a judgement about whether the NQT had been given sufficient written warning he or she was at risk of not meeting the requirements and whether the action plan put in place was sufficiently supportive. You can imagine that, in extreme cases, there is a risk the situation may lead to litigation on the part of an aggrieved NQT.

Aside from the NQT who is at risk of failing to meet the requirements of the induction period, another situation that needs to be handled with great care is where an NQT is completing the induction year in a series of temporary posts of one term or more. Clearly, the challenge here is to ensure the NQT has a coherent training programme that recognises his or her progress but also supports him or her as he or she equips him or herself with the necessary skills and knowledge for each new post. We would suggest that, in these circumstances, it is even more important to take the lead from the NQT and to use the CEP as an instrument for continuity.

Mentoring as a core professional skill

Throughout this chapter, a number of references have already been made to the idea that mentoring is no longer an optional extra in the repertoire of skills teachers have. It is an essential core attribute. This can be illustrated with reference to the linkages between ITT, induction and performance management. Within each of these three areas the mentor has a critically important role in facilitating the professional development of others. We also argue that the term 'mentor' is problematic because it means so many different things to different people. Its application within ITT, induction and performance management is slightly different whilst still involving a common set of skills and qualities. It follows that, whilst every school will be involved in performance management, if a school is not involved in ITT, this will mean the involvement of that school in induction will lead to an enhanced rate of development in mentoring more generally.

We wish to consider in a little more detail the nature of these linkages because it will help contextualise your role as induction tutor. Mentoring in ITT has developed rapidly over the last decade as there has been a move towards school-based training. It began in secondary schools with Circular 9/92 (DfE, 1992) and in primary schools with Circular 14/93 (DfE, 1993). Both these circulars sought to shift the emphasis away from higher education into schools. Higher education institutions were required to develop partnerships with schools for ITT, which included the transfer of funding to schools. These partnerships were reinforced by subsequent legislation that encompassed both primary and secondary phases. Circulars 10/97 (DfEE, 1997) and 4/98 (DfEE, 1998) established further the concept of partnership. Circular 10/97 (DfEE, 1997), for example, suggested that, for all ITT courses, there should be an obligation for schools and higher education institutions to work in partnership.

During the 1990s there was an extended debate about partnership and associated issues of resources, which challenged the autonomy of higher education and the role of teachers who were receiving students. We would wish to agree with Glenny and Hickling's (1995) observation that this debate obscured the benefits of partnership as

Section Three

realised through the development of mentoring. According to these authors, the reforms in ITT resulted in 'a rather truncated debate about partnership, focused primarily on the allocation of power and resources between schools and higher education, and [this] has obscured the more fundamental shared core purpose of improving the quality of teaching and learning for children' (*ibid*., p. 56).

That core purpose was directly related to the proliferation of mentor-training courses that occurred in the 1990s in order to support the new concept of partnership. Underpinning these courses was an assumption that a key element of successful mentoring was concerned with articulating own practice to student teachers. This in turn ensured a high degree of self-analysis, which related directly to enhancing the quality of teaching and learning.

It is possible to identify a range of key mentoring skills that are also central to your role as induction tutor. These can be defined as follows:

- **The whole activity is set within a national standards framework. In the case of ITT, these are the standards for the award of Qualified Teacher Status (QTS). In the case of induction, these are the induction standards.**

- **Observation and the provision of written critiques are a central element in both ITT and induction. Moreover, the skills of observation can be generically defined. Observation should be focused on specific aspects of teaching and learning, using an appropriate pro forma. Written critiques should be open and honest, but constructive and supportive. The whole process should be done with, not to, students and NQTs.**

- **Professional dialogue based on observation should be the key to effective mentoring. In both ITT and induction, a key part of this should be the review of professional objectives and the devising of action plans that take forward professional development and facilitate the student's/NQT's practice to grow and develop.**

- **The assessment of both the NQT and the student should be evidence based, fair, rigorous and valid. It should be grounded in the national framework but should allow for the exercise of professional judgement.**

We have made some links between the skills needed for effective mentoring in ITT and in induction. It is worth while to reflect for a moment on some differences. That there are differences in different forms of mentoring is reflected in the tendency to replace the term 'mentor' with a range of different terms for various circumstances. One ITT institution, for example, uses the term 'associate tutor' to describe the lead mentor in the school, whilst in induction the term 'induction tutor' is used widely. Moyles *et al.* (1998) itemise some of the difference in mentoring in ITT and induction. One is that the nature of the relationship will differ. In ITT the student is yet to qualify and, in a formal sense, the mentoring relationship is hence between someone who is as yet outside the profession. In induction, the mentoring relationship is with someone who has qualified, who is being paid and, therefore, by implication accepts professional responsibility. Likewise, the nature of assessment will be different. In ITT there will be a specific and, in many cases, detailed assessment against a large number of standards for the award of QTS. In induction, the assessment will, in most cases, be much more broadly based against groups of standards.

It is true there is a common mentoring skill base across ITT and induction. It is also true these common skills of observation, setting professional objectives and assessing practice are apparent in various roles within performance management. Look at the following quotation from the DfEE (2000a), which outlines the role of the team leader in performance management. You can see the same core skills again. First there is the setting of professional objectives for the teacher by the team leader. Then there is the requirement to observe and to gather a range of evidence for a review of these objectives. Whilst there are no national standards there is still a national framework, and this is expressed in the bullet that requires objectives to be focused on both professional practice and pupil progress. There is also a requirement for regular professional conversation focused on these objectives. Whilst it is true the relationship between the team leader and the teacher will be different from that between the induction tutor and the NQT, it is also true there will be many similarities.

The team leader must:

- **meet with each of the teachers for whom they will be the reviewer before or at the start of the performance management cycle and discuss setting objectives;**

- **record objectives in writing and allow the job holder to add written comments if they wish. Teacher objectives must include those relating to developing and improving teacher's professional practice and pupil progress;**

- **monitor performance against these objectives throughout the year, and observe the teacher teaching in the classroom at least once during the review cycle;**

- **consult the reviewee before obtaining oral or written information from others relating to the teacher's performance;**

- **meet with the teacher at the end of the performance cycle to review performance and identify achievements, including assessment of achievement against objectives, and to discuss and identify professional needs/activities;**

- **write a professional review statement and give a copy to the reviewee within 10 days of the final performance review meeting, and allow 10 days for the job holder to add written comments;**

- **pass the completed performance review statement to the headteacher (*ibid.*, p. 12).**

You can see why we reach the conclusion that the mentoring roles and responsibilities that apply to induction apply equally clearly to other contexts. For some, mentoring will be a career path with different mentoring foci at various times. For all, mentoring and being mentored will be an integral part of the role of teacher. The role of the induction tutor is part of a much wider context.

Section Four

Benefits and costs of induction tutoring – a concluding remark

As you read through this chapter you should have a sense of the responsibilities you will be accepting as an induction tutor. You may well be thinking these are fairly demanding and this is indeed the case. It is important, therefore, to balance this perception with a perspective about the benefits of being involved in induction tutoring. These are many. For yourself, you are developing and applying a core professional skill. You are also enhancing the quality of your teaching. For by articulating the essence of your practice to your NQT you will be providing yourself with the opportunity to reflect on your practice. In this way it is arguable there is a direct relationship between mentoring and pupil achievement. Should there be more than one NQT in school, or if you are sharing the induction tutoring of a single NQT, you will be influencing whole-school development. The dialogues you will be having with NQTs and your colleagues about effective practice will create a learning school ethos where reflection becomes the norm.

It is naïve to say that there are no costs associated with this role. It will involve a commitment of time, although it is possible to put in place strategies to manage this. It does involve the completion of additional paperwork and the making of arrangements for your NQT. It carries with it an awesome responsibility in relation to the influence you have over a new teacher. It can be particularly demanding if you have a failing NQT, where the scrutiny of your practice will be heightened.

However, we would argue that the benefits outweigh the costs. Not to be involved in the mentoring role denies opportunity for self-reflection and analysis. Not to be involved as a gatekeeper to the profession denies responsibility for the next generation of teachers and children. It is true the role of the induction tutor raises the stakes for both you and the NQT. It is equally true that, unless those stakes are raised (in a moderate and reasonable way), some crucial opportunities for your professional development will be denied.

In this chapter you will find material to support you in the following areas:

- **what you need to know about in order to prepare for the induction year;**
- **your thinking about the nature of high-quality teaching and learning;**
- **the current regulations in England;**
- **the Career Entry Profile;**
- **the characteristics of effective induction practice and producing a school policy on the induction of newly qualified teachers.**

Introduction and chapter overview

The opening chapter of this book established an overview of the scope of the roles, responsibilities and tasks an induction tutor might be required to undertake in the course of this work. The word 'scope' is used because we feel it is sensible to gain a view of the big picture. You can't do all this at any one time! Some parts you will be confident about, others less so. However, one thing is likely – if you have been invited to take on this work, accept it as a professional compliment. Newly qualified teachers (NQTs) only get one chance to be a first-year teacher! So don't be put off by what looks like an enormous job. Much of it you may well do already and many of the skills and abilities required you will use in the normal course of your work.

It will not escape your notice there is an enormous overlap with this work and being a curriculum leader, whether it be key stage co-ordinator, subject leader, head of department or head of year or, come to that, any post that involves management and leadership!

Being clear about what is expected and required is half the battle, and this chapter seeks to help you gain a confident grasp of precisely that. But also remember this is not a one-person job. Everyone can and should contribute.

There is some emphasis here on promoting high-quality learning and teaching and for those induction tutors who are fortunate enough to work in schools where this is the overriding, explicit and actively pursued purpose of the school, you are on a winner! However, there are currently several excellent books in this field and it is not our intention to replicate them here. We seek only to signal that any new teacher will benefit greatly from working in a school where the culture is characterised by the relentless pursuit, fascination and excitement of exploring learning and teaching issues.

So this chapter provides some material to help you understand much of the key knowledge and many of the skills and qualities required to be an effective induction tutor. It focuses on the links between your understanding of high-quality teaching and learning and the effective mentoring of NQTs, on the current regulating framework for induction and the nature of effective practice in induction, including the Career Entry Profile (CEP).

The fundamental aim of the chapter is to affirm that effective induction tutoring demands more than mere compliance with the underpinning rules and regulations. It requires you to be explicit about your understanding of teaching and learning.

Section One

Key elements in preparing for effective induction tutoring

The scene is now set. There's a worthwhile job to be done and we have discussed the range and scope of the *roles* an induction tutor may take, and we have considered the main *responsibilities* this work may include. It is clear that, in general terms, such roles and responsibilities relate strongly with other roles of curriculum leadership, such as key stage co-ordinator, head of department, advanced skills teacher, etc. However, we feel that, before undertaking any job or development in school, it is crucial to pose some short questions:

- **What is expected of me (as an induction tutor)?**
- **Why is it important to invest time in this (the process of induction tutoring)?**
- **How will I know if I am successful?**
- **How will I go about being an effective induction tutor?**

In schools where these questions are not addressed with precision, and where the leadership and culture of the school fail to provide the culture for the work to be undertaken, the chances of successful outcomes will be poor. There are countless instances where the failure to address the first three of these questions and jumping straight to the fourth have resulted in frustration, stress and little benefit for anyone.

These are important questions you can't answer alone. When headteachers ask colleagues to become induction tutors, they must ensure the circumstances exist to ensure effectiveness and success. We all need to know precisely what is expected of us, and the first three questions above need to be addressed *before* embarking on the fourth!

Given we are clear about what the work of an induction tutor entails, the logical question to address now is to do with the *knowledge*, *skills* and *qualities* that will support such work (see below). The remainder of this chapter, therefore, goes on to consider a number of these elements at some depth. Others not considered directly here are discussed elsewhere in this book.

What does an induction tutor need to know about?

- The scope of the roles, responsibilities and tasks of an induction tutor.
- High-quality learning and teaching:

  – a precise understanding and vocabulary about high-quality learning and teaching, especially in translating the standards for the award of Qualified Teacher Status and the national induction standards into a range of classroom strategies;

  – a working knowledge about learning styles and learning theory;

  – a repertoire of strategies that work in classrooms;

  – where in school high-quality teaching and teachers are located.

- Knowledge about the current regulations and the process of monitoring, supporting and assessing NQTs using the CEP.
- The characteristics of good practice in the effective induction of NQTs.
- Knowledge about the process of classroom observation.
- Knowledge about the school's culture, policies and systems.
- Knowledge of strategies for helping an inexperienced colleague.
- The skills and qualities needed to be effective.

We would like to start by thinking about the link between induction and high quality in teaching and learning.

The nature of high-quality teaching and learning

Section Two

At the end of a three-day training programme for induction tutors, one young teacher observed: 'This is the first management course I've attended and it's been really helpful.' It is interesting to note our colleague regarded this as training in *management* and she quickly made the links with other aspects of her work as a subject leader. The main business of schools is to provide high-quality learning and teaching for pupils and students. That is, after all, the ultimate aim of management (Shipman, 1990).

When the time comes to make the transition from initial training to that first teaching post, Qualified Teacher Status (QTS) should mean the new teacher is well prepared in content and theory and that the national standards for initial teacher training (ITT) as laid down in DfEE Circular 4/98 (DfEE, 1998) have been attained satisfactorily during teaching practice placements.

Induction tutors must be aware of those standards throughout the year. During the first term of the induction, the new entrant is to be assessed against these standards for *consistency*. The standards are a useful source of reference – which is a good way to think of them. It would be inappropriate to follow them slavishly as some sort of tick list. They should be used to inform progress and success as well as to provide clarity on expectations where the NQT has deficiencies or areas for development.

One danger of producing lists of standards is that they may be seen as an end in themselves. The standards may be seen as a pronouncement of good practice but may not be accompanied by any precise, shared understanding about how it might look in the classroom. This, of course, was one of the problems with teacher observations in teacher appraisal in schools, where there was no agreed policy on teaching and learning and where there was no whole-school agreement on the characteristics of effective practice. In essence, high quality in teaching and learning goes beyond meeting any one set of standards.

So, if there is one single unequivocal knowledge requirement for induction tutors, it must be they are confident in their knowledge about what makes for high-quality learning and teaching and how theory informs this.

One way we can do this is to take a precise look at some of the ITT standards that relate to planning teaching and class management and to ask ourselves the following questions:

- **What would we see the NQT doing/saying that would tell us the activity relating to this standard is taking place?**
- **Why is it important this takes place (i.e. in terms of the learning process)?**

When we begin to address these questions individually or, better, collaboratively, we can, through precise discussion, develop a shared understanding of what effective classroom practice should look like. Such discussion takes us all to a higher plane of mutual understanding. As Judith Little (in Fullan and Stiegelbauer, 1991, p. 78) finds in her school improvement research in Ontario, progress is more likely to occur where 'teachers engage in frequent, continuous and increasingly concrete and precise *talk* about teaching practice'. By such talk, teachers build up a shared language adequate to the complexity of teaching and capable of distinguishing one practice and its virtue from another.

Imagine, if you will, the potential richness (on a course or in a school) where 20–30 experienced teachers turn their minds to such matters. To see and hear teachers talking about what they do best is both exciting and humbling. Such talent and experience need to be unlocked and used for the benefit of us all.

We talk so often about expectations: high ones, low ones or sometimes a complete absence of them! The list given above about what an induction tutor should know is, of course, not exhaustive – but it seems to generate and develop the precise discussion a profession should demand. Given recent national pronouncements, many teachers could be forgiven for lapsing into a response rather than taking the initiative for themselves.

NQTs engaging with the consistent achievement of the ITT standards

Planning, teaching and class management

4(a)(iii) Setting appropriate and demanding expectations for pupils' learning, motivation and presentation of work.

4(k)(xiii) Setting high expectations for all pupils, notwithstanding individual differences, including gender and cultural and linguistic background.

What would you see the NQT doing/saying that would tell you this is taking place?

- Speaking frequently to pupils about his or her genuine belief in their ability.
- Not resorting to banal time-filling tasks, such as word searches.
- Setting crisp deadlines for tasks – referring to the classroom clock.
- Differentiating tasks and deadlines to suit individual needs.
- Always having higher-level extension tasks to hand.
- Talking about 'abilities' rather than 'ability'.
- Explaining the idea of multiple intelligence to pupils (parents and colleagues) and being positive about all types of ability.
- Planning lessons using a learning styles framework.
- Planning lessons using a differentiation model such as *must – should – could.*
- Giving pupils choices in how to tackle a piece of learning – perhaps two, three or four options based on different learning styles or language levels.
- Setting individual learning targets and behaviour targets with pupils.
- Being energetic, optimistic and upbeat in the classroom.
- Modelling high standards him or herself – being in the classroom on time, being prepared, keeping records up to date, taking relative risks.

Above we have identified and described some of the things we might expect to see an efficient NQT doing or saying consistently in relation to one or two standards.

This is much more concrete and specific – it unravels the standard and makes sense of it. More importantly, it invites collaboration – teachers talking about what they do best, what they are expert in. From this analysis, the next question that takes us into a realm of deeper understanding is 'why'? What do we know about learning and teaching theory that makes us say, for example, that 'speaking frequently to pupils about your genuine belief in their abilities' or 'planning lessons using a learning styles framework' are important? Who says so? Where's your evidence?

To answer this question, it is important to take note of the wealth of work on *learning styles*. It has often been a criticism of teachers that they tend to teach in the way they themselves prefer to learn. This can lead to teaching that lacks variety and that may disenfranchise up to 75% of the learners!

There is a wealth of research that links knowledge of learning style to successful learning outcomes. Here are five selected maxims that have stood the test of time:

- **Learners perform best in their own learning style (Shipman and Shipman, 1983).**

- **When learners are taught in their own particular style, their motivation, initiative and results improve (DeBello, 1985).**

- **The ideal method is to introduce the topic in the preferred learning style of the learner and then, for maximum benefit, to engage the learner in as many other processes as time permits (Wlodkowski, 1985).**

- **Learners score 'significantly higher' in a way that fits their own learning style (Trautman, 1979).**

- **Some 75% of teachers are sequential, analytical presenters; 70% of students do not learn in this way (Jenson, 1995).**

(For further reading in this area, see the end of this chapter.)

Whilst it is not the purpose of this book to replicate work on learning styles and the exciting current literature on the workings of the human brain, it would be remiss of us not to make some links between good practice in attaining the ITT standards and examples from learning theory. This is important because we argue that effective induction tutoring is dependent on an understanding of what constitutes high-quality teaching and learning.

Theory and practice

Gregorc's work provides an example of theory that can be used to inform curriculum planning and practice, especially with regard to differentiation by learning style. Just as importantly, our knowledge about learning styles can inform our work and relationship with newly qualified colleagues. Gregorc's research (Tobias, 1994) was based on the question, why do so many pupils fail? He came up with the continua shown in Figure 2 to represent the dual aspects of processing information.

The first continuum relates to the varying ways in which we *acquire information*, and this contrasts the concrete with the abstract approaches. The second continuum is concerned with how we *store information*, and here a logical sequential approach contrasts with a random organisation of information. Both these continua relate, of course, to us as induction tutors, our NQTs and the pupils we teach.

Gregorc found that, using his framework, there are four main types of learner:

1. **Abstract sequential**   about 27% of the population.
2. **Abstract random**   about 27% of the population.
3. **Concrete sequential**   about 27% of the population.
4. **Concrete random**   about 18–20% of the population.

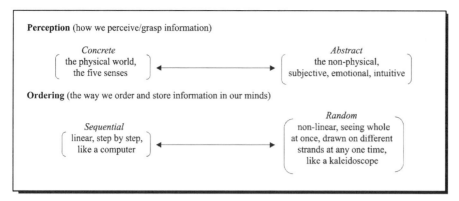

Figure 2. Gregorc's continua.

These go across all age ranges, abilities, socio-economic backgrounds, races and gender in roughly these proportions. There are some obvious implications for teachers when planning for their pupils' learning. Each of these types is characterised by pre-ferred ways of learning, and Figure 3 outlines tendencies for pupils who fall within each of the four categories.

Gregorc's model provides us with a very useful view about how our minds perceive and understand information. He identified *perception* and *ordering* as the two planks upon which his theory is based.

Perception is about the way we take in information and view the world. It is our perceptions that shape what we think, how we prioritise and make decisions. Our minds possess two perceptual qualities. These are *concrete* perception and *abstract* perception. Concrete perception lets us register information through our five senses – the here and now, the tangible. Abstract perception allows us to visualise and develop ideas. This quality involves us using our imagination, intuition and intellect. Of course, we all use both these qualities but are more comfortable using one rather than the other.

Ordering is the plank that is about the way we use the information we perceive. Gregorc contends that, once we have taken the information in, we all use two methods of ordering what we know. The two ordering abilities are *sequential* and *random*. Sequential ordering reflects a step-by-step, linear approach. It implies a logical train of thought with, perhaps, a plan. Random ordering permits our minds to organise information in pieces without any particular sequence. Random ordering is likely to be impulsive or spontaneous.

Put together, Gregorc's definitions give four combinations of the strongest perceptual and ordering abilities. No individual is one style only. We all have a dominant style or styles that give us our uniqueness.

(Figure 3 gives some of the words most often used to describe these dominant learning styles.)

Abstract sequential		Concrete sequential	
reading	sit down and work	hands on – doing	reading for a purpose
writing	lectures	things	maps, diagrams
note-taking	libraries	structured	lists
reasoning	essays	step by step	rules
structured analysis	quiet research	data and figures	tried and tested methods
		checklists	specific answers
		clear instructions	tangible outcomes
		attention to detail	
		computers	

For the pupil
You like reading
You are happy to work alone
You like to find things out from books, from talks and from other sources
You weigh up different ideas
You are keen to do written work
You organise your studies carefully

For the pupil
You like to do practical work
You like to be told exactly what to do
You like to tackle things one step at a time
You like to be organised
You pay attention to detail
You like to get things right

Concrete random		Abstract random	
problem-solving	originality	groupwork	co-operation
investigation	simulations	games	intuition
ingenuity	few restrictions	personalised work	self-expression
independent study	own timetable	relationships	up and doing
risks	up and doing	own ideas	imagination
open-ended questions	practical	emotions	peer teaching
and tasks	connected to the real	spontaneity	art, drama
curiosity	world	flexibility	discussion
	trial and error	stories	

For the pupil
You like to be given problems to solve
You like to work out answers for yourself
You have lots of ideas
You like to try your ideas out even if other people think they are odd
You like to find out how things work
You like to have something to show for your efforts

For the pupil
You like to talk things through with other people
You use your imagination a lot
You understand how people feel
You like to use drama, art and music
You like your work to be fun
You like your work to be about people

Figure 3. Four learning tendencies informed by the research of Anthony Gregorc.

Implications for induction tutors and NQTs

There are at least two implications from this theory. First, it is possible to apply the four learning tendencies to NQTs. Your NQT will, according to Gregorc, have a preferred learning style and it will be important you know what this is so your tutoring is effective and efficient. Just as you would differentiate your teaching for pupils, so you need to do this for your NQT. Your NQT's learning style may well contrast sharply with the NQT in the next class or school. Secondly, it is important that, as an induction tutor, you give some thought to finding out the preferred learning style of your NQT.

As a teacher and as an induction tutor, it is clearly vital you can confidently explain the learning process. Much has been written and researched about learning styles, and we know that some styles strongly conflict with others (Parsloe, 1993). For example, some people like the 'big picture' before they start in a school. These are the 'holists'. Others prefer a more measured, logical sequencing to arrive at the big picture. These are the 'serialists'. Others prefer visual approaches; others prefer to listen, talk and discuss. These are the 'visualisers' and 'verbalisers'. It is important an induction tutor knows about preferred learning styles before acting as a mentor for others.

Peter Honey and Alan Mumford (1986) have greatly influenced current thinking on learning styles, concluding from their research there are four main learning styles:

1. **activists;**

2. **reflectors;**

3. **theorists;**

4. **pragmatists.**

Activists like the company of others and enjoy full involvement in new experiences. They are open-minded and enthusiastic and are prepared to take risks. They have a tendency to become bored easily and enjoy thriving on challenge.

Reflectors enjoy looking at all the angles. They will do their research and find out the facts before jumping to any conclusion. They have a tendency to be cautious, are thoughtful and often may not contribute to meetings. They observe and listen and may appear distant.

Theorists enjoy thinking logically, in sequence. They tend to be perfectionists and will invest energy in analysis. They like ideas to be grounded in principles, theories or models. They also tend to be detached and seek objectivity rather than anything subjective that is likely to make them feel uncomfortable.

Pragmatists enjoy trying out ideas, theories and techniques to see if they work. They are always on the lookout for new ideas to take away and practise. They llike to get down to business and tend to become impatient with open discussion. They are practical, down-to-earth people and enjoy problem-solving.

Most of us can accommodate two or three of these styles with, perhaps, a strong dislike for one particular style. Honey and Mumford (*ibid.*) have developed a questionnaire technique that allows you to identify how strongly you prefer each of these styles. In their book, they suggest ways of developing your less preferred styles in order to maximise on opportunities.

Whilst there are inventories and diagnostic tools for this, an informal conversation and a developing relationship can reveal information about preferred learning styles. Overleaf are the responses from a group of induction tutors who were asked to reflect upon ways in which they prefer to learn.

- I like to be given relevant information which I can then fit into the processes already in place in my school.
- A variety of approaches from independent learning through to collaboration with colleagues/experts.
- Being analytical/applying learning to real problems.
- Video presentations again with discussion.
- Supported practice and written material.
- Lectures focused upon disseminating good practice.
- Groupwork – led from the front.
- Combination of professional expertise with applying theory to practice.
- Listening, watching.
- Lectures.
- Simply a variety.
- Small-group discussion (tutor led).
- Reflecting.
- Practically – minimal writing.
- Small-group/paired work, some reading, some observation.
- Through an appropriate mix of hands-on and taught sessions.
- Attending well planned courses, sharing models of good practice, 'having a go'.
- Discussing with others, putting ideas into practice.

This is both interesting and important. By inviting colleagues (in this case prior to a course) to give some indication of their preferred learning styles, we signal this is important. The information can be used in two ways. First, it provides a stimulus to develop thinking about teaching and learning. Secondly, it informs course design and delivery – when we reflect upon the above list, it is clear a variety of preferred learning styles are indicated.

By using pre-course information about colleagues, training providers mirror good practice – i.e. finding out about 'learners'. Good teachers try hard to cater for the range of learning styles. There is clearly a parallel here with designing a programme of induction for your NQT. What is important to consider is the preferred learning style of that colleague because this will inform how the process of the support part of his or her programme during the induction year will be managed.

Section Three

Regulations and the process of monitoring/supporting/assessing NQTs

The previous section asserted that, to be an effective induction tutor, you must have an understanding of high quality in teaching and learning, and the notion of preferred learning style should be one part of this. We now move on to consider what you need to know in relation to the national framework for induction.

A good place to start is the overview of the induction process produced by the Teacher Training Agency (TTA) because it implicitly gives pointers to good practice. Figure 4 gives a very clear picture of the process and of some of the important events that must happen with regard to the three key areas of monitoring, support and assessment.

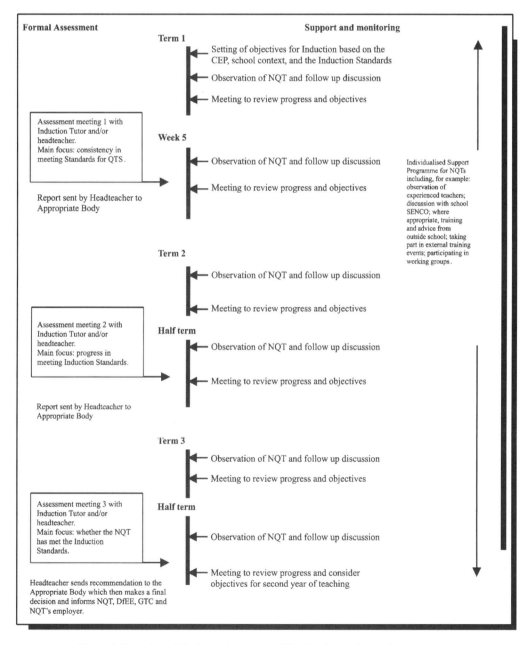

Figure 4. Overview of the induction process. The timeline indicates the key stages in the induction periods as set out in the circular. *Source*: TTA (1999).

This very helpful diagram provides a clear, at-a-glance 'helicopter view' of the induction year. You can see there are three key strands:

1. support;

2. monitoring;

3. assessment.

These are the three cornerstones of the induction year and none should be seen as more important than the others. The diagram illustrates the bare bones of what needs to happen and when. Obviously, there are 'major' general implications here for schools. These appear to fall into the following areas:

- **Having a policy for continuing professional development – including induction.**

- **Clear roles, responsibilities and tasks for the key players.**

- **Designated induction tutors.**

- **Regular informal and (six) formal observations.**

- **Opportunities for the NQT to observe other experienced teachers and to work with the SENCO (the special educational needs co-ordinator).**

- **Ensuring continuity with ITT, initially through the CEP.**

- **Formative and summative assessment against national standards.**

- **Review/progress meetings (at least six).**

- **A reduced (10%) timetable for the NQT and opportunities to attend training courses.**

- **Training and support for induction tutors.**

- **Provision for monitoring/evaluating the quality of induction arrangements.**

In essence this means the school ensures everyone involved understands what is required for induction, and there is a process to manage support, monitoring and assessment. Additionally, key staff must have the attitudes, knowledge and skills to undertake the roles, responsibilities and tasks associated with this aspect of continuing professional development.

Section Four

The Career Entry Profile

The Career Entry Profile (CEP) (TTA 2001) is a formal, statutory document and one which all NQTs in England are expected to complete. It was introduced by the TTA in May 1998 and has subsequently been refined. Apart from the statutory nature of the profile, it has the potential to be a very effective tool in promoting the transition from ITT to induction. However, this will only be the case where ITT institutions, ITT students/NQTs and schools give it the attention it deserves. For an induction tutor, the profile should be seen as a potentially very valuable document that will inform his or her challenging work.

SECTION B

Newly Qualified Teacher's strengths and priorities for further professional development during the induction period

This section should be agreed by the provider and the trainee teacher. Please refer to pages 8 and 9 of the Note of Guidance when completing this section.

Areas of strength in relation to the Standards for the Award of Qualified Teacher Status

1. *I have very good subject knowledge in mathematics which was my first degree subject. I am able to apply this subject knowledge very well to designing and implementing well matched tasks in numeracy in Key Stage 2. (Standards section A)*

2. *I am able to very quickly establish good relationships with my classes through being explicit about my expectations of children's learning applying these very clearly in practice and dealing calmly but assertively with deviations from this. (Standards section B)*

3. *I understand the idea of assessment strategy and am able to plan for the assessment of pupils' learning over the course of a period of time which identifies key moments for formal assessment. I feel particularly confident with this in numeracy. (Standards section C)*

4. *I am able to build very effective working relationships with colleagues and believe that I am a very good 'team player'. In particular I made a very positive contribution to the weekly team planning meetings during my final block placement. (Standards section D)*

Figure 5. An example of a completed Career Entry Profile (section B) for Michael Wright, who is completing a PGCE in the 5–11 age range.

SECTION B (CONTINUED ↑)

Areas in which the trainee teacher will benefit from further development during the induction period.

1. *I attended a taster course in geography during my initial training but need now to develop further my teaching within this subject, particularly the integration of map skills with geographical themes. (Standards section A)*

2. *During initial training I had a tendency to devise learning objectives which focused on what children would do, rather than what they would learn. This needs further attention during induction. (Standards section B)*

3. *I wish to build on the experience gained during initial training in reporting to parents. In particular I need now to develop the skill of writing reports which are both honest and positive. (Standards section C)*

4. *I wish to broaden the range of assessment techniques I use within science to include concept mapping. (Standards section B)*

To be completed towards the end of the ITT course, when decisions about the award of QTS are imminent.

Signature on behalf of ITT provider		Date
Name	**Job Title**	
Signature of trainee teacher		**Date**

To be completed following recommendation of the award of QTS

Signature on behalf of ITT provider		Date
Name	**Job Title**	

Figure 5 (continued). An example of a completed Career Entry Profile (section B) for Michael Wright, who is completing a PGCE in the 5–11 age range.

CEPs have two main purposes:

1. To ensure all NQTs have an individual path of professional development, which takes account of strengths and weaknesses as measured against the standards of the award of QTS. People are unique and have personal experiences. Falling into the trap of assuming all NQTs need the same things is analogous with failing to consider the individual learning needs of pupils in the classroom! The profile will inform the mutual setting of professional objectives – especially in the first term of induction – and provides the induction tutor with a tool to use in the early part of the relationship.

2. To ensure that monitoring, support and assessment are effective. These are the three main pillars of the induction year. Because the profile is a formal statutory document, it should mean the student leaves ITT with a very clear idea of specific strengths and areas for development. The profile links closely with the standards for the award of QTS and the national induction standards and, of course, during the first term, the NQT's performance against these standards will be assessed for consistency. However, the standards provide, as we have seen, enormous potential for stimulating discussion in teaching and learning which, in turn, will inform areas of focus for support and subsequent monitoring towards the achievement of objectives. It is important to note the profile will not be used formally to assess the induction period.

There are three sections to the CEP, labelled A, B and C. Sections A and B are completed prior to a trainee leaving ITT, whilst section C is considered in the induction year itself. Section A consists of a brief overview of initial training and includes reference to the course type, training provider, subject and age-phase specialisms, as well as to the distinctive features of both the courses and the trainees' professional biographies. In section B, the trainee identifies strengths and priorities against the QTS standards prior to leaving training. During the induction year, section C is used to act as a way of focusing the NQT's professional development through a process of action planning and the setting of professional objectives. Figures 5 and 6 show completed examples of sections B and C of the CEP.

Some headteachers are now inviting NQT candidates to bring their CEP to selection interviews, if they have been completed. In many instances where interviews are held well before the end of the summer term, there is no reason why schools that are informed about the CEP should not use it to inform the selection process (for example, by thinking about interview questions/activities). You may wish to use the standards framework and invite observations by the panel on areas of strength/areas for development.

NQTs who take temporary/supply teaching work before applying for a permanent post

It is worth remembering that some NQTs may, on leaving their initial training, take employment as temporary teachers or perhaps as supply teachers. Whilst there is

SECTION C

Objectives and action plan for the induction period

Once they have completed training, NQTs should consider their strengths and priorities for further professional development in order to prepare for their first teaching post, their induction programme, and their longer term continuing professional development. Once in post, this section should be completed jointly by the NQT and the induction tutor. Please refer to page 8 of the Notes of Guidance, the Standards for the Award of QTS on page 12 and the Induction Standards on page 20 when completing this section.

OBJECTIVES	ACTIONS TO BE TAKEN AND BY WHOM	SUCCESS CRITERIA	RESOURCES	TARGET DATE FOR ACHIEVEMENT	REVIEW DATE
To ensure that I am fully compliant with the school policy on assertive discipline.	• Seek briefing from the Deputy Head on the school policy. • Acquire and read background material on assertive discipline. • Implement the policy as quickly as possible with my class.	• Children understand that I apply the assertive discipline policy in a way consistent with other members of staff. • Lesson observation by Mr Cole confirms this.	• Time for meeting with DH (½ hr). • Background material and reading.	Sept 2001	Dec 2001
To develop my ability to design well focused lesson objectives which focus on children's learning.	• Professional conversation with Mrs Kay, Y6 teacher. • Gain feedback on lesson objectives planned in w/c 6th November. • Make lesson observations explicit to children.	• Lesson objectives are deemed to be focused in formal professional review meeting. • Children understand lesson objectives.	• Time for focused professional conversation (½ hr). • Time for feedback on lesson observations (½ hr).	Dec 2001	Dec 2001

Signature on behalf of employer	Date	Signature of NQT	Date

Figure 6. Michael's Career Entry Profile: part of section C.

unlikely to be any formal record of evidence of assessment in such instances, it is reasonable to infer the NQT will have benefited from this experience and will therefore have progressed since the ITT summative report was written. Interviewers would seek evidence of such progress.

The characteristics of effective induction practice and producing a school policy

Section Five

Whatever development we embark upon, it is prudent to take notice of good practice. Long before the Labour government of 1998 sharpened the focus on the induction year, there was a wealth of enlightened and successful practice in the UK and around the world. However, this has always been varied and inconsistent, and government edicts will not guarantee effective practice or consistency in the future. People are more important than systems. The quality of the induction process for NQTs will depend, to a great extent, upon several important preconditions:

- the culture of the school;
- the level of understanding of induction quality and leadership, especially by the leadership team;
- the motivation, knowledge and skills of the induction tutor;
- the motivation and level of NQT involvement;
- the permitting circumstances afforded by school leadership and the organisation;
- the resources, in terms of staff, time and funding.

The single most important message to emerge from school improvement research over recent years is the crucial role played by the *culture* of a school. Culture is about how people think, act and feel. It is the very essence, the day-to-day character of a school. It is to do with high-quality leadership: how people are treated, how they are involved, how they are trusted, how they are given responsibility. It is also about how seriously the headteacher who claims 'the staff are our most important resource' creates a learning environment for the staff as well as for the pupils. In this instance it is about the school's approach to continuing professional development – and, in particular, how the school discharges its responsibilities for ensuring NQTs experience an induction year that is informed by the characteristics of effective practice.

Our experience of working in this field over the last 25 years yields a range of understandings about induction. There is a continuum that seems to range from 'Just tell us what we have to do in order to satisfy the DfEE' to 'How can we ensure we provide the best possible start for our newly qualified colleagues?' It is also worth noting that when induction tutors are invited to say or write something about how they have come to be involved in a training course, there follow responses that range from 'I've been sent' to 'asked to look after', 'asked to see to' and the majority response that revolves around their professional motivation, the worthwhileness of such work and a wish to ensure their previous practice is developed for the future in the light of current research – policy development.

Being an induction tutor is not work to be undertaken lightly. It requires a high degree of motivation, skill and knowledge. However, these are not confined to this role and are, of course, eminently transferable to other curriculum leadership roles. The significance of this is self-evident.

By the same token, induction is a collaborative venture, and the NQT is responsible for being a proactive partner in the process. Professional development is not something 'done' to a teacher. We do not develop staff – rather we provide the environment, the permitting circumstances for a colleague to develop. In the case of an NQT, this means creating a range of opportunities for professional growth. Some of these opportunities need to be managed carefully. This returns us to the first three questions posed at the beginning of this chapter concerning clarity, precision and a shared understanding of what is required for effective induction.

Induction tutors are not there to 'look after' a newly qualified colleague. To describe the job in such terms is to misunderstand. The monitoring, support and assessment of an NQT are key functions calling for a sound knowledge base and well developed skills. This may require some opportunities for further training for the induction tutor – the financial resources for which are included in the funding now paid to schools for induction matters. It will certainly call upon the induction tutor's and others' time – time that is so precious and therefore needs to be used efficiently. Such efficiency emanates from a clear understanding of the requirements of induction and of the professional skills and strategies to make the process work.

The implications for you and for your school

As an induction tutor you might ask:

- **In order for our school to give our NQTs a high-quality induction year, what would it look like?**

- **What are we aiming for? In the past we have done our best but we want some reassurance about our past practice.**

- **We want to make sure we are up to date.**

These are typical of the comments made by colleagues embarking on work in this field. The saddest comment was the colleague who tearfully reported her own induction had been so appalling she vowed she would never let it happen when her time came to be a 'mentor'.

As with any developing practice, we need to know what we are aiming for and we need to know where we are starting from. There are some schools that have not employed an NQT for years and are, therefore, virtually starting from square one. Other schools have staff who are very experienced in mentoring ITT students and

NQTs. Some large schools may have a dozen or more NQTs. Whether it is one or twelve, one thing is certain. Each individual NQT will only get one chance to be a first-year teacher — and so this places a prime responsibility on the school to make it successful.

It is good management practice to establish a clear and accurate understanding of where your school is starting from. What is the current situation in your school with regard to the induction of NQTs? When you know the precise answer to this question, you have a clear understanding of what needs to be done. Is it a big undertaking or a small one? How great is the school's performance gap between where it is now and where it wants to be? Figure 7 provides a simple diagram that demonstrates this gap between the existing and preferred situations with regard to NQTs. The size of the performance gap will vary from school to school and may be related to a number of factors, such as unfamiliarity with the new regulations or not being involved with NQTs for some time.

The pro forma on the next page is designed to help you establish an accurate picture of the current situation in your school with regard to the induction of NQTs. It will help you to understand the size of the performance gap in your school.

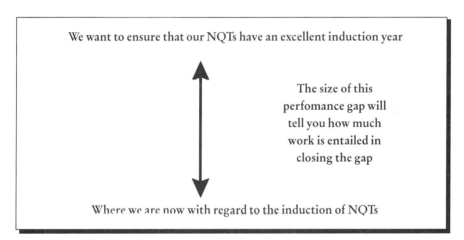

We want to ensure that our NQTs have an excellent induction year

The size of this perfomance gap will tell you how much work is entailed in closing the gap

Where we are now with regard to the induction of NQTs

Figure 7. The performance gap.

For some schools, the gap between current and desired practice is small. For others, it may be great (e.g. a school that has not employed an NQT for several years). However, it is important to be precise about existing practice in your school in order that you know the magnitude of the development required. To help you to do this, use the pro forma to audit the existing situation in your school. You are invited to grade each statement according to the extent to which it has been fulfilled. Remember also it is important to gain the views of others. This audit is best undertaken with another colleague at the school — even last year's NQT. You can of course use it to inform the development of a policy document for induction in your school.

Auditing the school's provision for the induction of newly qualified teachers

Best practice from a range of sources, including HMI, TTA and DfEE	The existing situation in your school (comment and grade)
The school has a policy statement on induction linking the induction of NQTs to the school's policy for continuing professional development and INSET that is informed by DfEE Circular 0090/2000 (DfEE, 2000c) and TTA materials on induction.	☐
The school has clearly written roles and responsibilities for those staff involved in the induction year (e.g. head, mentor/induction tutor(s), NQT), whilst acknowledging induction requires a whole-school approach.	☐
NQTs are allocated a designated person who has the knowledge, skills and qualities to engage in monitoring, support and assessment.	☐
Regular informal and formal observation of NQTs teaching – with follow-up discussions (a minimum of two formal observations per term).	☐
Ensuring continuity with ITT through the use of the Career Entry Profile.	☐
Opportunities for NQTs to observe other experienced teachers teaching in our school/in other schools and other work (especially with the SENCO).	☐
Training for mentors/induction tutors with some timetable relief to allow them to work with NQTs in the classroom.	☐
Making assessments on NQTs' teaching against national standards.	☐
Professional review of progress at meetings with mentor/induction tutor and/or head (at least twice a term).	☐
A planned induction programme of monitoring/support and assessment responding to individual needs and informed initially by the Career Entry Profile.	☐
A reduced timetable (10% less than a normal teaching load) and opportunities to attend training courses.	☐
The school makes provision to monitor and evaluate the quality of its induction arrangements.	☐

Grades 1–4
1 = This criterion fully met
4 = The school does not meet this criterion

Producing a school policy on the induction of NQTs

What – another policy? How can you justify the need for yet another policy? Our response to this relates to *purpose* and *audience*. Throughout this book you will find many thoughts, ideas and references that relate to the *professional reasons* for undertaking this work, the potential benefits, the roles and responsibilities of all parties and some strategies to make the good practice we know about come to life.

We all understand that the school has a statutory responsibility in this work – but that is no guarantee of effective practice! So we believe a well written policy, arrived at *with* the staff in a school, will provide a solid base for striving to achieve a consistent high-quality induction for NQTs. The policy needs to be succinct, clear and accessible to staff, governors and others who are interested in how a school manages continuing professional development.

Your school may already have a policy that covers this area of work. Good practice in all parts of an organisation's work – ensuring there is time built in for periodical review – may be all that is required (a structure you could use for such a review is given below).

Drafting an induction policy

1 **Guiding principles and rationale**

- Why have a policy (some professional reasons; how it fits with the culture of our school; some legal reasons)?
- What are the intended purposes and outcomes of the policy (for the NQT; for the induction tutor; for the school – including pupils!)?
- In what ways is the policy informed by good practice and how does it relate to the provision the school makes for initial teacher training?

2 **A brief statement on the identification and support of the needs of NQTs**

- Using the Career Entry Profile.
- What we know about generic needs.
- The importance of the needs of the individual.

3 **Personnel**

In our experience, any development stands or falls on the precision about who will do what. Who are the key personnel who will have *roles* and *responsibilities* in this area (e.g. headteacher, induction tutor, NQT, all staff)? What will they actually *do*?

4 Finally, ask yourselves this question: in what ways will the school's culture and management provide the permitting circumstances for this policy to be translated into action?

If you do not have a policy or you want to start again, it is a simple matter to draft out a policy to discuss at a staff meeting or with a group of staff interested in continuing professional development. We have deliberately not written a policy here, primarily out of respect for the reader! However, the structure we offer may help your school to make an individual response. Obviously, the parts of this book that resonate with your context and philosophy can also be useful in shaping your response. This will give purpose and clarity to your work, and you can inform your policy by referring to the excellent TTA materials (1999) on *Supporting Induction of Newly Qualified Teachers*.

It is important not to confuse a policy with a programme. Whilst it is tempting to draw up a comprehensive programme of monitoring and support at the start of induction, it is important to remember we are dealing with individual needs as well as the needs of the school. Programmes should be negotiated with individuals but will also take into account the work of the school. For example, a new colleague will need to know about writing reports on pupil progress and the practice of managing parent meetings. The secret is to get the timing right and not to overburden a new colleague with everything all at once!

Reviewing your existing policy

It is good management practice to review our work. This tells us how we are progressing in relation to what we have agreed to do. The table opposite shows some prompts to help you review existing practice.

Conclusion

Before we move on to the next chapter, we wish to ask two key questions:

1. What should a school do?

2. What is good practice?

In 1978, a policy was prepared on the probationary year for a brand-new high school. As part of the rationale for this policy, a reference taken from the McNair Report produced in 1944 was included:

> The damage done to a young teacher by his taking a first post under a personally unsympathetic Head, or one who has no understanding of what the training institutions aim at doing, may be irreparable, and such tragedies can be prevented only by a properly organised system of probation which is regarded as a continuation of the teacher's probationary period (*ibid.*, p. 24).

It is amazing that it has taken over five decades (since McNair, the work of Bolam, the James Report and teacher induction pilot schemes) for us to have finally arrived at an official entitlement for NQTs.

When we consider the McNair quotation, we realise there is now a well thought-through system for the induction year, and there is no reason why anyone should be ignorant of the ITT standards. They are there for all to see and use – and, what is more, they are part and parcel of the CEP. So the transition from ITT to the induction year has the potential to be a smooth one in a way that has not previously been consistently managed.

Reviewing an existing induction policy	
Reviewing your existing policy	How your existing policy relates to this
Guiding principles and rationale When was the policy last reviewed, and what were the outcomes? In what ways does the policy communicate the professional importance of this aspect of CPD and link with ITT? Are the stated purposes of the policy being achieved? What evidence is there of this? In what ways has the policy used the evidence from good practice?	
The NQT What does the policy say about new teachers and in what ways does it demonstrate an understanding of their position and their needs?	
Current documentation How up to date is your policy? How does it relate to current TTA and DfEE standards and requirements?	
Personnel Who are the key personnel who will have *roles* and *responsibilities* in this area (e.g. headteacher, induction tutor, NQT, all staff)? What will they actually do?	
School culture What can you infer from the policy about the way in which the school's culture and management will provide the permitting circumstances for this policy to be translated into action?	

Learning and teaching: selected further reading

Armstrong, T. (1999) *Seven Kinds of Smart: Identifying and Developing your Multiple Intelligence*, New York: Plume Publishing, Penguin Putnam.

Dryden, G. and Vos, J. (1997) *The Learning Revolution*, Auckland, New Zealand: The Learning Web.

Hughes, M. (1999) *Closing the Learning Gap*, Stafford: Network Educational Press.

Jenson, E. (ed.) (1995) *The Learning Brain*, San Diego, CA: Turning Point Publishing.

Jenson, E. (1998) *Superteaching*, San Diego, CA: The Brain Store.

Scottish CCC (1996) *Teaching for Effective Learning*, Dundee: Scottish Consultation Council on the Curriculum.

Shaw, S. and Hawes, T. (1998) *Effective Teaching and Learning in the Primary Classroom*, Leicester: The Services Limited.

Tobias, C. U. (1994) *The Way They Learn*, Colorado Springs, CO: Focus on the Family Publishing.

Trautman, P. (1979) 'An investigation of the relationship between selected instructional techniques and identified cognitive style', in Jensen, E. (ed.) (1995) *The Learning Brain*, San Diego, CA: Turning Point Publishing.

In this unit you will find material to support you in the following areas:

SIGNPOST

- **good practice in managing the process of classroom observation;**

- **how to run productive meetings in the induction year;**

- **key interpersonal skills for induction tutors – listening and questioning;**

- **managing review and giving feedback;**

- **helping your NQT to set objectives and to plan for success.**

Introduction and chapter overview

We have now revisited the big picture with regard to good practice in induction and what an induction tutor needs to know. In this chapter, we sharpen the focus on the most important areas of monitoring and support. These are summarised in Figure 4 on page 27. Arguably, the single most important aspect of support and monitoring is *the quality of the management of the process of classroom observation*. Where this process is clearly understood and well managed, the opportunities for the development of all those involved are massive.

In schools where classroom observation is perceived as bureaucratic, unwelcome or as professional snooping for accountability purposes, there are likely to be few benefits in terms of higher-quality teaching and learning. Observing teachers teach in order to assess them against sets of standards, whilst serving a purpose, has very limited use and even less impact on young people.

However, we have already mentioned the notion of school culture and the vital importance of creating a culture where all teachers can grow professionally. We made reference earlier to the work of Judith Little (see page 20) and now do so again, for she also recorded that such improvement is also enhanced:

> When teachers observe each other teaching and provide each other with useful evaluations of their teaching – only such observation and feedback can provide shared referents for the shared language of teaching, and both demand and provide the precision and concreteness which makes the talk about teaching useful (cited in Fullan and Stiegelbauer, 1991, p. 78).

There are many schools where this is part and parcel of school life, and teachers are at ease with each other's presence in the classroom and use their skills, abilities and experience to inform practice.

Sometimes, in large schools, such a collaborative culture may be found only in certain departments. This clearly has implications for the newly qualified teacher (NQT) who works in a 'closed-door department'. Hence the need for induction to be seen as a whole-school issue and therefore to be well managed and co-ordinated to ensure consistency of opportunity. Otherwise, the situation can arise where the quality of one NQT's induction year in, for example, the humanities department may be very different from his or her colleague's experience in the science department. We accept that schools have within them micro-cultures, and this is healthy. However, what is untenable is the inconsistency of induction practice when it leads to poor experience.

It is important that we do not perceive our work to be in discrete parcels (i.e. this is what a head of department, a year co-ordinator does; this is what an induction tutor, a senior teacher, an advanced skills teacher, a special educational need co-ordinator, a head does). Of course, they all have their individual specialities, but high-quality teaching and learning should be the end for all their management efforts. And, therefore, it is not difficult to take a step back to make the links with the different aspects of the roles and responsibilities we all undertake in a school.

This chapter builds upon our earlier work on learning and teaching and sets out a process and some strategies for undertaking classroom observation and managing review and feedback. This is supported by a look at the key communication skills required. During the year, there are many different meetings to manage, and we provide some thoughts about ways in which these can be made effective. Finally, one natural outcome of observation is objective-setting, and we suggest some principles and approaches to this important issue.

Readers will note that much of this chapter relates to good practice as a curriculum leader in a school and will inform practice on what is currently termed 'performance management'.

Section One

The process of classroom observation

The induction arrangements (see Figure 4) inform us that an NQT must be *formally* observed at least twice every term and that the information gathered will inform termly assessments. It is important to remember there can be many opportunities for an NQT to be observed *informally*, and such occasions have equal merit with regard to the potential for professional development through support and monitoring.

As a requirement, these formal observations are to be welcomed because it becomes an entitlement for the NQT that can provide opportunities for his or her professional growth. The emphasis here is on *can*, because the quality of outcome will depend upon the skills and understanding of those who manage the process of classroom observation.

Let us look first at the national requirements:

- **Observation shall occur at least once each half-term and within four weeks of the start of the first term.**

- **Notes on these observations should inform the basis for discussion with NQTs.**

- **In turn these should feed into professional review meetings.**

- **A range of people should observe the NQT.**

- **Observation should relate to the NQT's objectives and action plan and to the induction standard.**

There is a sensible logic and sequence to these requirements. At this stage in their careers, NQTs have the potential to learn much in a short time. Bolt-on, end-of-term check-up observations, undertaken because there is a form to fill in, are not likely to be an efficient or effective use of precious time. Research informs us that one characteristic of effective schools is they provide a learning environment for teachers as well as young people (Sammons *et al.*, 1995). And so the investment of time in classroom observation with the purpose of professional learning and growth goes some way to fostering and developing an important characteristic of school effectiveness.

Classrooms are fascinating places. Anyone who observes teachers in classrooms as part of his or her job quickly appreciates the value of reflecting on the whole complexity of classrooms and their own value positions. As teachers we never stop learning. As Hopkins (1997, p. 164) puts it, 'Good teachers have no ceilings'.

Why should we observe an NQT teach – what are the reasons over and above those required by the DfEE? Experienced teachers will typically make such responses as:

- **to encourage/support;**

- **to offer guidance;**

- **so you know what you're discussing;**

- **to learn;**

- **to look at a focus;**

- **to work on a weakness;**

- **to collect Information for assessment;**

- **to provide objective feedback;**

- **to look for weaknesses/strengths;**

- **to look at what the pupils are doing;**

- **to find out about relationships.**

These are what experienced teachers in primary and secondary schools think. They have been distilled from responses received over several years from many courses in various regions of the UK. We find them interesting and each one is ripe for amplification. For example, 'so you know what you're discussing' – as experienced teachers, it is no doubt *not* difficult to listen to an NQT's problem (or success) and respond appropriately and usefully. However, on the occasions when we were actually there inducting – seeing and hearing what was happening – it was so much easier to engage in precise discussion. Many experienced teachers mention that, through observation, they can learn not only *about* the NQT's practice and development but they can also learn *from* the NQT. As one induction tutor said: 'Induction is surely not just about helping teachers to cope. They bring with them a freshness of vision, perhaps even a naïve, unsettling, questioning, approach, which we can all learn from.' This, of course, reminds us the NQT has much to offer a school. We should always be mindful of this and seek to provide opportunities for his or her contributions.

In essence, these teachers have also teased out the key components of the process of observation – because it is a process. Omit any one of the three and the chances of a successful outcome are drastically lessened. Remember, there are *formal* and *informal* observations, and there are three components to the formal process:

- **preparation;**
- **observation and the collection of information;**
- **review and feedback.**

Preparation for observation

Both you and your new colleague need to be clear about the *purposes of the observation*. These may be wide-ranging but the bottom line is surely about helping an inexperienced colleague to grow professionally and to improve his or her effectiveness in teaching, classroom management and managing learning for young people.

As an induction tutor, especially to begin with, you might agree to observe your new colleague at work using an open agenda – looking at a range of aspects of teaching. The outcome of this is likely to be the sharpening of a focus on some specific areas for development. For example, during the first term of induction when the Qualified Teacher Status (QTS) standards need to be checked for consistency (see Chapter 4), you may agree to work on a specific initial teacher training (ITT) standard that would benefit from more precise consideration. For example:

> **5(e)** Encourage pupils to think and talk about their learning and to develop self-control and independence.

Or you may agree to focus on a specific teaching skill, such as 'giving instructions', 'effective questioning', 'responding to pupils' or 'setting expectations'. Of course, the scope is enormous and the specifics will depend upon the individual performance, disposition and needs of the NQT.

Whatever the purposes for the observation (which may include assessment), it is vital for both the induction tutor and NQT to be clear about these. Simco (2000, p. 49) considers these purposes from the viewpoint of the NQT and lists them as:

- an opportunity for you to receive feedback in relation to the targets which you have negotiated with your induction tutor through using the **Career Entry Profile** and to provide a context for review of targets;
- an opportunity for you to discuss your progress in the induction period using a specific lesson as a context;
- an opportunity for you to understand, through discussion, why certain aspects of your teaching meet with success and others are problematic;
- providing you with some reassurance that you are making steady progress towards the induction standards (or, in rare cases, informing you at an early stage that there is much to achieve if you are to meet successfully the induction requirements);
- providing evidence which can be used in the formal assessment meetings at the end of each term;
- an opportunity for you to establish possible new targets as you review your **CEP** at various stages in the induction period;
- an opportunity to gain feedback on your teaching from a range of perspectives (induction tutor, head of department, etc.).

For the purposes of illustration, John (an induction tutor) describes how he prepared for an observation:

> Early in the term Joy and I arranged a meeting to discussion lesson observations. Joy brought her CEP [Career Entry Profile] to this meeting. The purpose of the meeting was to discuss the rationale for the lesson observation process. I made it clear that the overriding objective was to help Joy to grow professionally and to optimise her effectiveness as a teacher. Joy welcomed the opportunity to have her lessons observed and felt it would be beneficial. It was agreed that since this was the first observation, it would be good to keep the areas of focus fairly general, but to use her CEP as a starting point.

Joy's CEP noted three areas in which QTS standards have 'been met, but where the trainee teacher will benefit from further development during the induction period'. These related specifically to:

(i) increased knowledge and understanding of Numeracy Strategy at Key Stage 3;

(ii) continue to improve her demonstration skills especially when working on the chalkboard;

(iii) ensuring end of lessons are purposeful and consolidate learning.

Following the review of Joy's CEP, the pro forma for the lesson observation was discussed. It was agreed that a sheet focusing on three areas of professional development would be used, so the meeting now concentrated on clarifying these areas. Prior to joining the school, Joy had attended numeracy strategy training at the school and had also spent time checking the students' level of attainment from the department's assessment arrangements.

The preparation discussion resulted in the following areas of focus:

- **use the three-part lesson structure at Key Stage 3 (as agreed as a result of the training day);**
- **use previous attainment to inform planning;**
- **use the chalkboard and a variety of teaching styles effectively.**

Clearly, all these relate to planning and practice, but the outcome of the preparatory conversation was that Joy was engaged in a process with purpose. John and Joy agreed on how John would observe:

> We agreed that I would use the agreed pro forma, as well as making other, more general notes, with the objective of providing useful information to inform our review. I would arrive at the lesson before the students, sit at an agreed seat at the side of the classroom during the main part of the lesson, but would move around groups when appropriate, helping pupils and asking them about their work. Joy would announce that I was there to 'see how they were getting along'.

In this instance there was a rigorous, professional conversation, which was useful to both colleagues and which resulted in a clear understanding about purposes and process. A preparatory meeting might last ten minutes or it may be considerably longer. It depends upon how far it becomes a planning meeting too! In the example above, the induction tutor referred to the initial standards for the award of QTS. As we noted in the previous chapter, these standards can provide a valuable stimulus for discussing teaching and learning and for focusing upon specific issues.

A further example is offered here. Again, rather than merely taking the standard as read, we have opened it up to give it more meaning. This time we have selected standards **5(e)** and **5(f)**:

> Many teachers, especially inexperienced ones, do not always provide pupils with enough opportunity to reflect on their learning in this way — and yet research informs us that the greater the opportunities to reflect and articulate our learning, the more likely the learning is retained (Hughes, 1999, pp. 21–59).

> **5(e)** Encourage pupils to think and talk about their learning and to develop control and independence.

> **5(f)** Encourage pupils to concentrate and persevere in their learning for sustained periods, to listen attentively and to talk about their experiences in small and large groups (TTA, 2001, p. 24).

What would you see the NQT doing/saying that would tell you this is taking place? Experienced teachers, when discussing this, came up with these suggestions:

- Taking time to explain learning objectives and how they relate to the big picture of their learning.
- Taking time to talk about, and evaluate, the learning process with pupils – not just intent on getting through the syllabus.
- Asking class how we can (collectively) and how they can (individually) do things better next time.
- Over time, giving pupils experience of different types of groups (friendship, random, mixed ability, mixed learning style, same gender, mixed gender, etc.).
- Over time, giving pupils experience of different resources (e.g. textbooks, the teacher, Internet, visits, each other, TV, organisations, etc.).
- Always sharing learning objectives and deadlines with pupils.
- Frequently asking pupils' opinions about how something should be tackled, how long it should take, how it should be presented.
- Offering pupils choices of learning activity (same learning objectives, but different learning methods based on different learning style and/or language levels).
- Using personal learning plans with pupils to structure individual project work and research.
- Setting SMART targets and deadlines with pupils and holding them to account.
- Organising resources so they are easily accessed by pupils.
- Changing learning activities often enough so pupils don't get bored.
- Guidance available in the classroom for: using a reference book; making notes; how to memorise; how to conduct a group discussion; how to redraft a piece of work; etc.

It is only when we begin to unpick these lists (i.e. when we engage in concrete, precise discussion about learning and teaching) that we remind ourselves of the fascination and enormity of the scope of the strategies available to teachers. It won't escape our notice that the standards for ITT are just as appropriate for teachers when discussing the key aspect of the work undertaken with pupils in classrooms! So the standards for the award of QTS are there to be used. They are a useful source and stimulus for talking about teaching and learning. However, they are not an end in themselves and, if used as such, the quality of outcome and discussion could be rather vacuous.

In order to achieve greater precision and shared understanding in the preparation stage for observation, we have found that the use of a simple 'focus wheel' has proved to be a valuable tool to inform and record discussions between the NQT and induction tutor. We find it is best used in A3 format. It is simply the hub of a wheel with segments drawn around it. The agreed focus is written in the hub and then discussion develops around that focus.

The discussion centres around what would be good practice and what you could do in the classroom. The purpose of this is to have a professional conversation about an aspect of teaching the inexperienced teacher is trying to develop within his or her repertoire. The outcome is a shared understanding of the focus, a written summary that can provide valuable information to help the NQT plan his or her work and knowledge that will inform the induction tutor's observing. For example, Geoff felt he needed to extend his understanding and skills when using questioning as a teaching technique. In the preparation session he and his induction tutor, Glynis, consider the wider issue of questioning in a way that would help Geoff to develop his skills and knowledge in these areas (see Figure 8).

The more we think about teaching, the more there is to break down. What we write in the hub is important. Perhaps it might only be appropriate to focus on 'techniques in questioning'. In this case, Geoff welcomed the opportunity to explore the subject with his willing and knowledgeable induction tutor.

However, we feel it important to offer a cautionary note here. Sometimes our own knowledge and enthusiasm can be overwhelming for the NQT, who may see the gap in his or her knowledge and practice depressingly large! So we suggest vigilance and sensitivity from the induction tutor – otherwise we run the risk of the NQT thinking 'This is more than I wanted to know about questioning!' or 'I could never do that'.

Figure 9 gives another example, where Vanessa is experiencing difficulty in using groupwork as a teaching strategy. With her induction tutor, Tony, she discussed some important aspects of groupwork and the focus wheel shown in the figure is the result. This discussion arose out of a previous lesson observation where the pupils did not understand what working in a group meant. Whilst the pupils were well behaved, they were unable to engage effectively in collaborative work because they had no ground rules and did not understand what was expected of them. This discussion with the induction tutor raised Vanessa's awareness of some of the key considerations that inform planning when using a potentially very powerful learning strategy.

All this is about preparation for an observation. You could be forgiven for thinking what a great deal of work this entails – but experience tells us that where induction tutors invest this time, they find the work more worth while. Observation to note professional development in a structured way does, however, take time. Where the observation is purely for assessment purposes alone (and even this is unlikely to have no professional learning as an outcome), the preparation is easier. At the crudest level, it could be the NQT is told he or she will be observed during lesson 3 next Thursday. The purpose is to assess, and a pro forma will be used and will inform the termly assessment. But teachers don't get taller by being measured as, indeed, neither do pupils. Of course accountability is important – but there are many more benefits to be gained by giving attention to careful preparation.

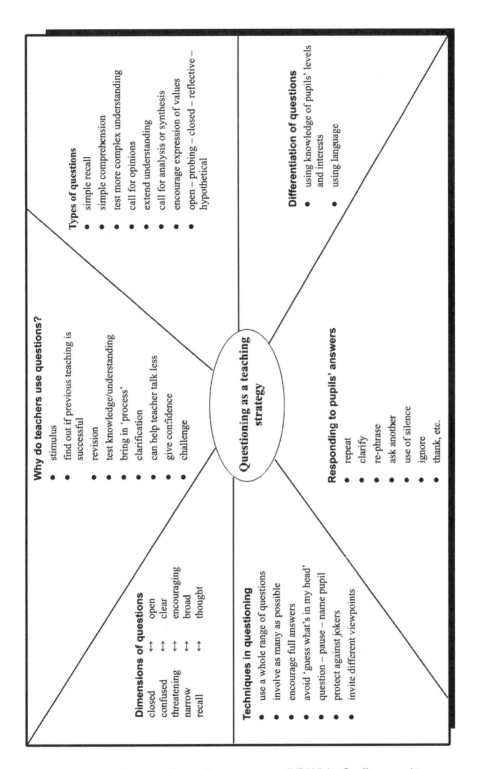

Figure 8. Using a focus wheel to explore questioning. (NB Whilst Geoff was teaching in a secondary school, variations on this focus will be important for teachers, whatever the age range of pupils/students.)

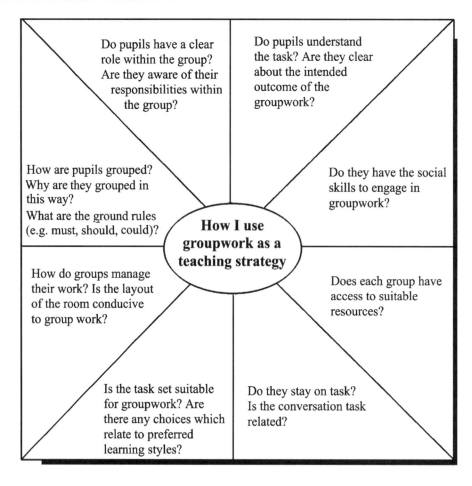

Figure 9. Using the focus wheel to explore groupwork.

Preparing for observations

Work collaboratively to ensure you both have a shared understanding of:

- the purpose of the observation;
- the precise areas of focus of the observation;
- using the CEP to inform early discussions;
- how the QTS and induction standards inform observation;
- any particular difficulties about subject matter, strategies or prompts;
- those aspects of teaching the NQT wants feedback about;
- which lesson and when;
- how the observer will operate;
- the observation pro forma to be used;
- what the pupils will be told;
- when you will meet to review the lesson;
- what documentation will be provided for the observer in advance of the lesson;
- how each other is feeling at this stage of the process.

Observing other teachers

Many headteachers will assert that the biggest resource in the school is the teachers. This assertion moves beyond rhetoric when the leadership of a school facilitates and nurtures a culture that permits the adults in the school community to learn – as well as the pupils. One strategy for enhancing teacher learning and for making use of the greatest resource in the school is to create systems and cultures that afford opportunities for teachers to observe each other at work. With regard to NQTs, this is partly recognised by the DfEE (2000c, para. 52):

> The NQT should be given opportunities to observe experienced teachers to help develop good practice in specific areas of teaching. This could be in the NQT's own school – or in another school where effective practice has been identified, e.g. in Beacon Schools.
>
> The focus for the observation should relate to the requirements for satisfactory completion of the induction period and to the NQT's objectives for development.

There can be pitfalls associated with NQTs observing experienced teachers, which include:

- **an overwhelming feeling of inadequacy ('I'll never be that good');**
- **a lack of understanding and receptivity of the observed teacher;**
- **the inability of the observed teacher to articulate his or her approaches ('I don't know why, I always do it like this');**
- **showing off;**
- **the NQT being seen by the pupils as the inexperienced teacher who has everything to learn;**
- **a lack of opportunity to discuss teaching and learning approaches with the observed teacher.**

The message here is self-evident. To make the best use out of observing another teacher, the following merit some attention:

- **prepare for the observation;**
- **enlist the support and involvement of the observed teacher over and above being observed;**
- **be confident he or she is willing and able to talk with precision about his or her work;**
- **ensure the timing is right for the NQT;**
- **ensure time is allowed for the NQT to review and reflect on the learning.**

It is easy to arrange for the observation of an experienced teacher at the wrong time, for the wrong reasons. Is it better for an NQT to observe a brilliant teacher who is charismatic and idiosyncratic and loved by all, or a teacher who is particularly adept at teaching a topic or using a strategy with which the NQT is grappling? We do not improve by osmosis. To sit an NQT in a classroom observing a brilliant teacher can be soul destroying. It could shatter confidence and it may or may not be an approach best suited to the NQT's own learning style. This is analogous to sending the head of a struggling school to observe a highly effective school. We might all be able to describe excellent teaching and excellent schools and it is not our purpose to devalue those practices in any way. It is how we close the gap between where we are now and where we aspire to be that is the challenge – and that is the essence of being an induction tutor.

What we seek to avoid is what one of our colleagues calls the 'Burglar Bill approach'. This means taking systems and strategies and attempting to translate them into another body, which will, of course, reject the 'new organ' unless the conditions are right.

For example, superbly executed groupwork managed in one school may not be immediately transferable to another unless certain conditions are satisfied which may be to do with the social skills of the pupils, their previous experience or even the layout of the furniture. The size of the performance gap between existing practice and aspired practice can be great or small. An effective induction tutor will help a new colleague to think through what was observed and the conditions that permitted the good practice. Deeper rather than shallower thinking will support the NQT's objective in developing teaching skills. However, there remains in education today (even at the highest levels) a foolish perception that we can improve by imitation.

Observing an NQT in the classroom

If the preparation stage has been well managed, the observation stage will be simple – but that is not to say easy! When we observe another teacher at work it is very easy to be critical to the point of thinking 'I wouldn't do it that way'. Earlier in this book we looked briefly at learning styles, and its worth thinking about this in relation to the observer, the observed and the pupils. There is always the danger of observing as a superordinate – rather than as a colleague. Show a video of a teacher teaching to a group of teachers and ask them to discuss without a focus and they will be very articulate about what is wrong. As teachers, it is sometimes difficult to be objective because we all have our own agendas, interests and values. Obviously, in schools where teachers talk a good deal about teaching and learning, there is a greater likelihood of shared values, understandings and expectations (of pupils and of each other). As long as we remind ourselves of the purposes of the observation, we will be well on the way to a worthwhile use of precious time. Teacher colleagues have summarised some of the lessons learnt from engaging in classroom observation as follows:

- be prepared in terms of both the purposes of the observation and the context of the lesson for the **NQT** *and* the pupils;

- be aware of the effect you may have as an observer;

- remember classrooms are complex environments and no one can observe everything;

- think about where you will sit and how you will act;

- beware of your own prejudices and of making snap judgements.

Who will observe the NQT teaching?

- The *induction tutor* is the person who is likely to undertake most of the observations of the **NQT**'s teaching. This is especially appropriate given that this is the colleague who is supporting professional development during induction.

- The *subject co-ordinator* in a primary school or the *head of department* in a secondary school will also need to observe. Many primary **NQTs** will have identified particular subject areas in sections **A** and **B** of the **CEP** where strengths and priorities for professional development are defined. This is often the case when a subject has only briefly been addressed in **ITT**. It makes sense for observations in these subjects to be the focus of actual targets. In secondary schools, a head of department's observation will be important within the main subject.

- The *headteacher* or *deputy headteacher* are most likely to observe an **NQT** at least once during the induction period.

- *LEA inspectors/advisers*, especially those with responsibility for co-ordinating induction arrangements, may be invited to the school. This will vary from authority to authority, but inspectors/advisers can provide a useful outside perspective in relation to the **NQT**'s teaching.

- *Other teachers* may observe, especially at the request of the **NQT**. One **NQT** invited the special educational needs co-ordinator (**SENCO**) to observe a lesson where there were several pupils who were working on a range of individualised activities. Other teachers may be invited and involved because they have a particular insight into an aspect of the curriculum (e.g. music/art/physical education).

Whoever observes, everyone must be aware of the school's approach to the process of classroom observation and must use this to inform his or her practice and to ensure consistency. In some large schools where there may be several NQTs, this work needs to be co-ordinated and managed if we are to assure quality and consistency of experience for our new colleagues.

Some approaches to observation

There are several approaches to classroom observation, ranging from the very formal 'headmaster's visitation' we came across in one school to the very informal 'drop-ins' encountered in another. It is, of course, fitness for purpose that is the most important consideration. It seems to us the most important outcome of the observation stage in the process is *to collect information objectively to inform a review of the lesson that will include discussion on the main focus, or areas of focus.*

Very sensibly, there is no nationally prescribed lesson observation pro forma. We have seen scores of variations produced by teachers which suit various purposes. These are the best – the ones produced and owned by the teachers who use them. Some experienced teachers find a blank sheet of paper all they need to record their observations. Others find a limited number of key areas or prompts helpful. Most teachers find an overly complicated pro forma inhibiting to the extent that filling in the form becomes more important than observing the teacher and pupils at work. This is fine as long as the NQT is clear about the purpose of the observation and if this strategy is likely to yield quality information for later discussion.

Again, we make the link here with preferred learning styles. The observer's preferred learning style may have an effect upon his or her preferred approach to recording information. However, as we see later, when the purpose of the observation is assessment, both the observer and NQT must be absolutely clear about the criteria to be used.

Some observations may be highly structured, seeking to gather quantitative information (for example, observation involving tallies of different types of verbal instructions between teacher and pupils). Our example of questioning techniques could lend itself to such an approach. Some quantitative approaches may be the outcome of earlier, qualitative, open-ended observations, such as those that may come during the first half-term.

The Teacher Training Agency (TTA) guidance on support and monitoring (1999, p. 10) is helpful here and states:

> Quantitative and qualitative approaches are not mutually exclusive and the selection of approach depends very much on the focus of the observation. Different approaches prompt different kinds of professional discussions and it can be helpful to use more than one kind of approach during the induction period. Experience of different approaches also helps the NQT to develop evaluative skills.

So the message is clear. There is no single pro forma. Fitness for purpose and flexibility are the key, and using a range of approaches will inform critical thinking. We include here three examples (Figures 10–12). For further examples that relate more precisely to learning styles and to the impact on learning more generally, a good source of information is Mike Hughes' book, *Closing the Learning Gap* (1999).

NQT INDUCTION	
Lesson Observation Record Sheet	
Newly qualified teacher	
Induction tutor	
Class and subject/topic	
Date and time	
Focus of observation	

Planning, teaching and class management

Monitoring, assessment, recording, reporting and accountability

Other professional requirements

Figure 10. Lesson observation record sheet.
Source: TTA (1999).

Name of teacher .... Class .... Date .... Time .... Activity .... No. in group ....

PROMPTS FOR USE IN CRITIQUE SHEETS	General comment (set context of lesson in terms of theme/topic/subject, desired learning outcomes, NC PoS covered, lesson structure/format)
A. Subject knowledge and application 1. Adequacy of subject knowledge for teaching. 2. Able to deal with pupil misconceptions. 3. Adequacy of knowledge and use of the National Curriculum/Desirable Outcomes. 4. Able to cope securely with subject related questions.	
B. Planning 1. Sets out clear and appropriate teaching objectives. 2. Incorporates NC PoS or agreed syllabus requirements. 3. Outlines a clear structure for the lesson that identifies tasks for individuals, a group and/or the whole class. 4. Caters for pupils who learn at different rates (is differentiated). 5. Includes opportunities to promote SMSC development.	*Issues to consider*
B. Teaching and class management 6. Sets challenging but attainable expectations for all pupils. 7. Ensures lesson objectives are met and pupils acquire/consolidate knowledge, skills and understanding. 8. Ensures a purposeful working atmosphere, sound learning and effective discipline. 9. Engages pupils and sustains interest and motivation. 10. Includes effective interaction (explanations, questioning, discussion) with the pupils.	
C. Monitoring, assessment, recording, reporting and accountability 1. Checks how well learning objectives have been met. 2. Provides constructive oral/written feedback to enable the pupils to do better. 3. Provides evidence of progress and for the setting of targets. 4. Helps the trainee teacher evaluate his or her own teaching to improve effectiveness. 5. Informs future planning.	*Targets for development and action plan* (to be completed in the tutorial)
D. Other professional requirements 1. Appropriateness of personal presentation for teacher role. 2. Responsiveness to health and safety issues. 3. Commitment to children reaching their potential. 4. Appropriateness of management of other adults in the classroom.	

Figure II. Lesson observation pro forma.

Teacher ……………………………..Class ……………………………………..Date………….
PLANNING AND PREPARATION (lesson plan, differentiation, catering for a variety of learning styles)
RELATIONSHIPS WITH PUPILS AND BEHAVIOUR MANAGEMENT (group, individuals)
TEACHING STRATEGIES (instructions, explanations, questioning, range and variety of approaches, plenary)
LEARNING AND RESPONSE OF PUPILS (pupil involvement, attitudes, responsiveness to different teaching strategies)
LEARNING ENVIRONMENT (suitability, display, room, resources)
OTHER COMMENTS (e.g. achieving lesson objectives)

Figure 12. Classroom observation sheet.

Section Two

Meetings

This section and the next reflect on the types of situations for which induction tutors need to be equipped with a range of interpersonal skills. They also offer some practical strategies to support you in being effective.

We begin with the different types of meetings in which you may be involved.

The variety of meetings

The meetings you may be involved in will have various purposes:

- **to prepare for observation;**
- **to review/discuss/give feedback on teaching;**
- **to review progress;**
- **to agree targets, and so on;**
- **to assess achievement against the national requirements (see Chapter 4).**

The effectiveness of these interactions will rely heavily on the quality of the induction tutor's interpersonal skills. The key skill areas include the abilities to:

- **listen actively;**
- **question;**
- **summarise;**
- **give feedback.**

Running productive meetings in the induction year

One of the problems with having management responsibilities in a school is there is no or at least very little time for managing because most teachers spend most of their time in classrooms with young people. It is therefore self-evident that teachers with management responsibilities must be excellent managers in order to make the most efficient and effective use of the small amount of time they have available. Unfortunately, they have to find and use time as and when they can, which is often before or after school or at break times and lunchtimes.

Increasingly in schools, headteachers are recognising that, if they are delegating management responsibilities to colleagues, they must strive hard to create the circumstances for the job to be undertaken. Many headteachers are creative at making time for their colleagues and realise that, for any delegated work, there are costs – in terms of time, money and energy. At the time of writing, there is funding for every NQT designed to offset the financial cost of induction.

There are several kinds of meetings that need managing during the induction year, many of which might be led by the induction tutor. These could include:

- meetings to prepare for lesson observation;

- meetings to review lesson observations;

- professional review meetings;

- assessment meetings.

When you have read this chapter, you should not have any difficulty in thinking about the planning, purpose and content of these four important types of meeting.

Meetings to prepare for classroom observation, review and feedback

Earlier in this chapter (page 45) we gave a summary of the key issues you may address during these informal meetings. These relate to purposes, strategies and the use of documentation. Use these to inform your meeting and you will both be well on the way to using your time well. Also use the TTA materials (1999, p. 7). In this chapter we suggest some skills you already use everyday that you can hone to help you carry out this work.

Meetings to review a lesson perhaps call for the highest order of interpersonal skills, and this chapter provides you with further support for this. But remember this is still a meeting – with a purpose and an intended outcome – so it is worth giving attention to the process of managing the meeting.

Professional review meetings

These are not the same as meetings to review a lesson observation. They cover a wider range of issues and should occur at least once every half-term. Good managers build in time for review so they can keep on track, make amendments, perhaps change direction and also speed up or slow down. Review is not assessment. These meetings, because they cover a wider range of issues than the ones described above, lend themselves to providing an opportunity for the NQT to contribute fully and to reflect with an experienced colleague on his or her professional development. These meetings are key features in the programme of monitoring and support and need attentive management. In this sense, whilst the approach may well be informal, these meetings are in fact a formal requirement and, again, the TTA materials (1999) provide suggestions on the planning and recording of these meetings. The professional review meeting is arguably the most important of all. It can provide a very important opportunity for an inexperienced colleague to reflect, with the skilful support of an experienced colleague, upon the previous six weeks' work. It calls for excellent meeting management and effective interpersonal skills.

The assessment meetings are three formal meetings once a term, and these are addressed in more detail in the next chapter.

Other meetings

Of course there will be many other sorts of meetings during the induction year that may involve, for example, informing the whole staff about the school's policy; seeking support from colleagues; meeting to co-ordinate induction where there are several NQTs; and discussing school-based INSET to provide training and support for NQTs and induction tutors.

All these can be effective if the process is managed well. This chapter helps you to do just that.

Why some meetings are a waste of time

We tend to feel well disposed towards meetings we consider to be professionally worth while. Think of the last meeting you attended. How did you feel on your way to it, during it and at the end? If you felt positive about it, the meeting was probably effectively managed! If you felt negative about it, perhaps it was characterised by one or more of the following:

- **there was no clear, shared purpose;**
- **there was no agenda;**
- **there was a poorly constructed agenda;**
- **more time was taken than was necessary;**
- **the meeting failed to achieve its purposes;**
- **colleagues were allowed to talk about anything;**
- **the meeting was too tightly controlled and discussion was suppressed;**
- **there were no ground rules.**

Who is responsible for addressing the above? Is it one person's responsibility or do others have a part to play? Perhaps if you experience meetings with these characteristics and are prepared to put up with them, then think again! We all have responsibilities for these and, by meetings, we mean two or more people! Time is precious, so we should not complain about the lack of it and at the same time permit others to waste it.

Of course, meetings matter, and they do not all need to be formal in the sense of procedural issues. But all the above characteristics could apply to a meeting between two people. Meetings matter because:

- **they can focus attention on, and give status to, for example, induction;**
- **we tend to support the actions, decision and plans we make with others;**
- **they can make us more accountable for what is agreed;**
- **they can help unfreeze fixed ways of thinking;**
- **they can generate new/more ways of tackling a problem;**
- **they can make people feel valued and supported.**

It is not difficult to make the links between this general list and the meetings that will take place during the induction year. Meetings can raise whole-school awareness and, indeed, challenge the odd cynic who had 'no fancy induction in my day'. Perhaps if he had, he wouldn't be a cynic! Many informal and informal meetings end with a summary of things to do. These may be formalised in an action plan. What is clear is that when we work collaboratively, we have ownership and with that may come responsibility – and accountability. A problem shared. On training courses, inexper-ienced induction tutors have often found that working with more experienced colleagues on issues that concern them has helped them enormously to see a way forward. This models the collaboration that should happen back in school. Finally, meetings can result in people feeling valued and supported as a consequence of their contributions to the meeting or, indeed, as a result of feedback on their work.

The purposes of meetings

Sometimes, colleagues might say a meeting was poor because no decision was made. Perhaps the purpose of the meeting was *not* to make a decision but to consider options. There can, therefore, be many purposes, and each agenda item could have a different purpose. For example, to:

- **review;**
- **make decisions;**
- **agree targets;**
- **assess;**
- **discuss;**
- **inform;**
- **plan;**
- **share.**

The list goes on and the message is clear. When you are meeting with a colleague or colleagues, be clear about the items for discussion and the purposes or intended out-comes.

Be ready – give some preparatory thought

A little thought and planning beforehand can make a world of difference:

- **Give attention to the *agenda*, however small.**
- **Agree it well in advance.**
- **Make sure anyone reading the agenda will understand what it means.**
- **Ensure others can contribute to the agenda.**
- **Careful construction: easy at beginning, difficult in the middle, non-controversial at the end.**

- **Ensure the sequence is logical, with continuity.**

- **Make sure you are well briefed.**

- **Think about the physical setting.**

- **Think about any teaching aids you might need.**

Whilst the above might seem like common sense, they may not always reflect our experience. Every day there are people in all walks of life attending meetings that have no purpose – maybe they have no agenda or it is received on the way into the meeting. However, think of the meetings you will participate in or lead during the induction year and you will make the links with your work as an induction tutor, subject co-ordinator or head of department.

The skills needed to lead a meeting

Whether it is a one-to-one or a larger group meeting, there are some skills good communicators can use to ensure an effective, worthwhile use of time:

- **how you start the meeting;**

- **questioning and listening;**

- **moving forward;**

- **summarising;**

- **keeping focused;**

- **testing comprehension;**

- **recording decisions/actions (which might mean objective-setting).**

We now move on to consider some of these skills in more detail.

<table>
<tr><td>

Section Three

</td><td>

Some key interpersonal skills to support induction tutors in their work

</td></tr>
</table>

So far in this book we have talked about such things as roles, responsibilities, good practice, preparing for and undertaking classroom observation, etc. All this is designed to help you appreciate the scope of the work involved in the induction of an NQT. However, the successful management of anything has more to do with people than systems (Everard, 1986, p. 128). The skills and ability of the induction tutor – as with any other management post in the school – depend upon high-quality communication skills. Many of the problems and frustrations that exist in all organisations or individual relationships can be traced to poorly managed, ineffective communication.

Here, we focus briefly on some of the skills that will help any teacher or other person to reflect upon and develop his or her effectiveness as a colleague who is helping another to grow and move forward professionally. There are four, key, basic skills that are essential. To:

- **listen actively;**
- **question;**
- **summarise;**
- **manage review and feedback.**

We have only to refer back to Figure 4 on page 27 – the overview of the induction process – to remind ourselves of the potential value of such skills. But these skills are not ends in themselves but means or instruments to be used in achieving helping outcomes (Egan, 1990).

Listening

To offer to another person your individual attention is perhaps one of the greatest courtesies we can afford to one another. Many people claim to be good listeners – and it has been my good fortune to work with a few who have exceptional skills in this area. I have also experienced many who do not listen but who are waiting to speak! They are often heard to utter 'I hear what you say ' and you wait for the 'but' (unless they have been on an assertiveness training course – in which case they say 'however'!).

We have asked our course members over recent years to describe what they see to be the important attributes of good listeners, and overwhelmingly the same ones surface:

- **They don't interrupt/or allow others to interrupt.**
- **They give you their undivided attention.**
- **They don't rush you or make you feel as if you are an irritant.**
- **They give you just the right amount of eye contact.**
- **They smile when it's appropriate.**
- **They are supportive in body language and in making affirmative noises.**
- **They are comfortable with silence.**
- **They are good at asking the right questions.**
- **They say things that tell you they have been listening.**
- **They are good at summarising or bringing things to a conclusion – however temporary.**

Again, these points are what experienced teachers have found. However, they are ideal characteristics and the context of the interactions may not be conducive to creating the perfect situation, especially in informal situations. They can, of course, be exploited where the conditions are appropriate.

Before we move on to examining the positive attributes of the good listener, our course members have found no difficulty in identifying the characteristics of poor listeners. In essence they are, not surprisingly, the opposite of the above list and can be distilled out into various stereotypes:

- **the fidget;**

- **the over-earnest;**

- **the know-all;**

- **the non-reactor;**

- **the inaccurate;**

- **the glassy-eyed.**

The *fidget* often gives off signals that he or she doesn't really want to spend time on this. He or she continues to shuffle papers, look at the computer screen or watch and does not give attention. He or she makes his or her colleague feel rushed and something of an inconvenience. The *over-earnest* can often be intimidating by trying too hard, making the speaker uncomfortable. Eye contact may be too much and questioning may become like the Spanish inquisition! Sometimes he or she completes your sentences for you! The *know-all* is a superficial listener who frequently doesn't hear the message behind what is said. He or she is often quick to come up with solutions, interrupts and gives little time. He or she may seek to impress with his or her knowledge and will not ask any questions. The *non-reactor* goes through the motions, nods at anything and everything but contributes nothing. It is possible that this type might play a useful purpose in some circumstances – but normally this will not help at all. The *inaccurate* is often a prejudiced listener and, sometimes, some of the words used make him or her switch off from listening, which results in a failure to understand. The *glassy-eyed* has his or her mind on other things or far distant places. His or her eyes glaze over, and often a dreamy expression appears on his or her face. The result is the speaker feels negatively towards the 'listener'.

As listeners, we should be aware that most people can think about four times as fast as the average person speaks. Thus, the listener has three quarters of a minute of spare thinking time for each listening minute! Sometimes this 'spare' time is used to think about other things, concerns, troubles, instead of listening, synthesising and summarising what the speaker has to say. Listening, therefore, demands a high level of concentration and skill.

Sadly, some of our colleagues go through their professional lives continuing to exhibit some of the characteristics of these stereotypes. However, it is important to remember that there are other barriers to good listening, apart from the most important ones (i.e. the skills and abilities of the listener):

- **the physical environment;**

- **the time of day: pressures;**

- interruptions;

- the listener's well-being;

- the listener's attitude to the speaker;

- the listener's attitude to the focus of the conversation.

Of course, these are self-evident. If we were asked to describe our ideal physical listening environment it might include things relating to space, comfort, heating, lighting, noise level, privacy, lack of interruptions, etc. High-quality listening is demanding. Anyone who has been involved in the interview process where several candidates are questioned and listened to over several hours will know about contextual inhibitors to listening. The disposition of the listener is an important factor in the equation, and his or her well-being can have a significant bearing.

For induction tutors (who used to be called mentors), the Chinese character for the verb *to listen* is worth exploring briefly (see Figure 13).

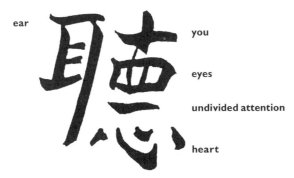

ear   you

eyes

undivided attention

heart

Figure 13. The Chinese character for the verb 'to listen'. This character gives an insight into the true meaning of listening. On the left is the *ear*; on the right are *you, eyes* and *undivided attention*. If it is understood that 'hearing' means one thing, 'listening' means giving attention to the speaker, using his or her eyes and internalising what he or she is saying.

Questions, and helping colleagues to talk

Effective listeners are skilled at questioning, and 'good questions get good answers'. Earlier in this chapter we used questioning as a teaching skill (see Figure 8), and it is possible to see the relevance of this to our work as induction tutors.

As an induction tutor, it is important not to fall into the trap of *telling* your NQT what to do or what not to do. Obviously, if it is a matter of pupils' safety at stake or an agreed school practice or protocol that is at issue, then telling may be appropriate, even essential. Helping a colleague to reflect, evaluate, make connections, plan, etc., is better achieved by *asking* him or her about thoughts, actions, intentions, feelings, etc. However, beware of asking so many questions your NQT feels grilled! This will not help your relationship.

We ask questions to gain information about something, and we can ask different types of questions (see Figure 14). *Open questions* are a good way to get the conversation underway. They are designed to elicit some general information that will provide a basis for further discussion. For example, one induction tutor in a planning meeting with her NQT asked: 'There are several topics and approaches for you to choose from. *Tell me about* the areas that interest you most.' Similarly, following a lesson observation, an induction tutor will often ask: 'It was really good to see you at work. *What pleased you* about the lesson?' These are general questions that can open up the conversation. In our funnel diagram (Figure 14), open questions may often lead to more questions.

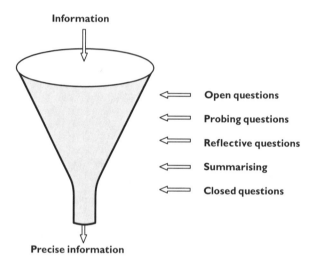

Figure 14. Questions to support a review conversation.

Probing questions fill in the details. Sometimes they may simply require a look of surprise, interest or the raising of an eyebrow that can give the speaker a cue to say more. Alternatively, it may be a question such as 'How did you decide on that?', 'What happened?' or 'What evidence do you have?' Probes can keep your new colleague from rambling or being vague.

Reflective questions are also a means of obtaining further information. As the name suggests, they reflect back to the speaker something he or she has said or implied: 'You said you find Natalie difficult – why is that?', 'You say that was disappointing?' or 'You didn't expect that to happen?'

Closed questions are important, but if we only ever ask closed questions we will gain very little insight or information and might be unable to help the speaker reflect. Closed questions fill in the details and require simple factual, quantitative, affirming answers: 'Did they understand the task?', 'How many completed the task?' or 'Were you satisfied you achieved your purposes?'

Summarising is another key skill. Good communicators use this well. Summarising keeps conversations on track, whether they are one-to-one or in a meeting. Summarising can occur many times in a conversation or a meeting and can be used to clarify and record the progress made in a conversation. For example:

> So if we can just pause for a moment. With regard to your work with this class, you have good, sound evidence of their progress; you are pleased with your developing relationship, and now feel confident to use some more 'risky' strategies with them, especially role play. Is that a reasonable, accurate summary so far?

Managing post-observation meetings, progress review meetings and the processes of review and feedback

Section Four

Meetings between an induction tutor and an NQT following a lesson observation will vary according to the perceived purposes of the conversation. Sometimes, people talk about 'feedback' and 'giving feedback'. This is important, and research confirms that the brain needs feedback from its own activities for the best learning and growth to take place. However, there is a danger in regarding review and feedback as *separate* processes. The classic failing of mentors, therefore, is only ever to *give* feedback. While this can be very useful, it might also be telling someone something he or she already knows. At the other extreme, *review meetings* will help the NQT to reflect and make sense of what he or she did. The skilful induction tutor, therefore, will manage a review conversation that weaves in opportunities to give feedback, and it is this model we support.

Figure 15 illustrates a process which many induction tutors and others who observe lessons have used successfully to plan and carry out a post-observation conversation, which is the third component of the process of classroom observation (see page 69).

The purposes of a post-observation review meeting

Post-observation review meetings have many purposes:

- **to acknowledge strengths;**
- **to develop confidence;**
- **to note areas for improvement;**
- **to offer advice;**
- **to explore/offer strategies/alternatives;**
- **to encourage self-reflection.**

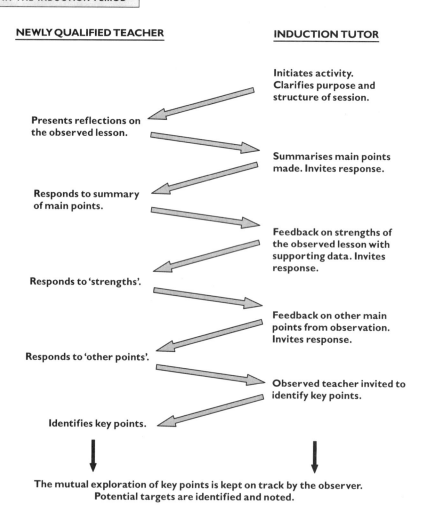

Figure 15. Managing a post-observation conversation.

All these are laudable and realistic intended outcomes. Many of today's teachers have lived and worked throughout a period when their confidence levels have been severely tested and, in some cases, diminished or shattered. Confidence is a fragile commodity at the best of times, and many a new teacher has had his or her confidence dashed by some unthinking comment in the staffroom from a colleague or at the school gate from a parent. So we should therefore look for every opportunity to help a new colleague to recognise and affirm strengths, for it is only by registering these successes that we gain our confidence, which leads us on to explore and practise alternative ways of working.

Many teachers with responsibilities for supporting others have not been trained to manage review, to give feedback or even to receive feedback themselves. For induction tutors, these are key areas for practice and development. First, we offer a tried and tested structure for a review conversation. This includes providing feedback – a topic we develop further later in this section.

As noted above, Figure 15 provides a way through a post-observation conversation. The observer leads and sets the scene for the conversation – sketching out a structure. It is fairly typical to invite the NQT to present his or her general reflections on the lesson. There is always the danger here, however, of the NQT listing a catalogue of inadequacies. Teachers can be very self-critical. So it is important to seek to achieve a balance at least between the positive and negative, although it is understood that, on some occasions, this may be very difficult!

This opening part of the conversation can set the scene for the rest of the conversation, which will become more precise as it flows on. The induction tutor may then respond to these general reflections by summarising them first. For example:

> So, overall, you're saying you are much happier with the way this class behaved; you achieved what you set out to do and you managed the resources much better. You are still concerned about the last ten minutes of the lesson and the quality of the homework produced. Does that sum up your initial thoughts?

Having invited the NQT to respond, the induction tutor might then move deeper into the discussion about the lesson and offer some thought about what was observed and recorded. This may include statements such as:

- **I liked the way you greeted the class and had the resources all ready to hand.**
- **I think a real strength of your teaching is your creativity in designing interesting activities for your pupils.**
- **The group by the window responded very well and were 'on task' for most of the time.**

Such statements may invite further comment from the NQT, thereby helping to develop the skills of reflection and concrete, precise discussion about teaching and learning. The induction tutor should be able to refer to actual data or information gathered – whether making positive or negative observations. As long as they are constructive observations, they will be appropriate.

After the NQT has responded to a summary of strengths (and has not been permitted to deflect compliments!), the conversation may move on to the other main points observed – some of which may be weaknesses or areas for development the NQT has articulated earlier. These will involve further discussion and summary, and are likely to provide the ingredients for *objective-setting*. Whatever you do, it is essential to encourage the NQT to identify what has been learnt from this conversation process and to be specific about it.

Good practice dictates that the NQT and the induction tutor have a copy of the summarised conversation. This provides a useful record for both – and, of course, provides documentation to inform a progress review meeting and the termly assessment meeting.

Thinking about feedback

During the late 1980s, a group of teachers in Cumbria, working on Pupil Records of Achievement, identified some key factors that promote effective learning:

- **I need to have feedback: what I can do well, what I need to improve and my progress.**

- **I need to recognise my own achievements and have these recognised by others.**

- **I need to know what is expected of me.**

- **I need to have some short-term, achievable targets.**

- **I need to feel valued and respected.**

- **I need to be offered strategies to help me learn more effectively.**

- **I need to be able to evaluate my own learning and to develop my own strategies to improve it.**

If this is the case for young people, in what ways does this list relate to the NQT? Does this reflect in any way his or her potential needs? Clearly, there are some transparent and transferable links between young learners and adult learners. They represent fundamental needs and, of course, are inextricably bound up with theories of motivation. In fact, we would venture to say that the list applies as much to headteachers as it does to pupils!

Feedback is not an end in itself. It is a skill that can be learnt and developed, and we see it as integral to the process of review. The giving and receiving of feedback can generate a sense of risk for both parties. Effectively giving and receiving feedback implies certain key ingredients: caring, trusting, acceptance, openness and a concern for the needs of others.

Some NQTs may be defensive about receiving feedback, and this raises the challenge of helping them to use it for their personal improvement. It is important to remember that, regardless of how accurate feedback may be, if an NQT or any other colleague cannot accept the information because he or she is defensive, feedback has little value. Feedback must be given so the person receiving it can *hear* it in the most objective and least distorted way possible, can *understand* it and can choose to *use* it or *not* to use it (Shtogren, 1980). You will note that in the model (Figure 15) we provide opportunities for the NQT to respond to feedback – whether positive or critical.

There is sometimes a problem when the NQT *deflects* or *distorts* the feedback. Professional humility is all very well but do not let the NQT deflect and reduce positive feedback. Equally, if you feel he or she is distorting feedback, giving an opportunity to comment can help to clarify in your mind his or her understanding or interpretation of your feedback.

Receiving feedback

Turn the situation on its head and think about some guidance for receiving feedback. This is important for all of us and, obviously, there are skills we can bring into play to help maximise the experience. The following are some general suggestions that, no doubt, we could all make use of:

- *Listen*: give yourself time.
- *Question*: check your understanding.
- *Decide*: it is helpful, valid; if not, you can reject it.
- *Respond*: decide how to act; be open not defensive.
- *Ask*: for the feedback you want but haven't received.

Of course, an NQT is in a very different position compared with established colleagues. NQTs are assessed each term, and this may affect how they may respond.

In most cases, where the induction tutor's feedback is informed by these points, mutual evaluation becomes a natural outcome. It is, once again, the difference between *asking* and *telling*, between *review* and *feedback*. Reading a list of positives and negatives from a clipboard has limited value and will usually tell the NQT about what he or she already knows. This will not promote reflection and the critical analysis that leads to improvement. Most inexperienced teachers can ably describe the weakest aspects of a lesson – which, of course, makes your job of helping them to develop strategies and skills to improve the weaker aspects of their teaching much easier.

When you give feedback it is worth considering these points:

- Be explicit and specific.
- Offer feedback on what you observe.
- Start with the positive.
- Be descriptive rather than evaluative.
- Focus on actions that can be changed.
- Choose which aspects are most important and limit yourself to those.
- Ask questions rather than make statements.
- Think what it says about you.

Explicit feedback gives the receiver some clear information about the effect of his or her work; it means that that person no longer has to guess about or make assumptions about the effect of his or her behaviour on others. Offering feedback on what you observed can help to bring objectivity to the conversation. For example: 'It was ten minutes before the group on the table at the back of the room started working' or 'When I talked with your learning support assistant, she understood precisely what you wanted the group to be able to do by the end of the lesson'. These are factual comments that can be discussed further. Most observed lessons are likely to be at least satisfactory and will always provide opportunities to celebrate strengths or to identify areas for development or weaknesses that need working on.

Figure 16 shows the relationship between the degree of learning and the specificity of feedback. The more specific the content of the review or feedback, the greater the potential for learning. In our experience, most teachers are quick to point out their failings themselves. Often, the induction tutor has the job of helping them to keep keeping things in proportion! However, seeking to ensure precision in the conversation will enhance understanding and learning. Such feedback is more useful if it is given as soon after the event as possible but allowing enough time for individual reflection beforehand.

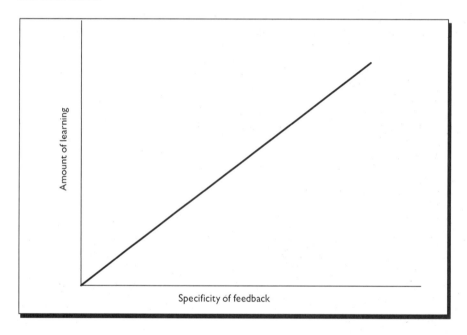

Figure 16. The relationship between the specificity of feedback and the amount of learning.

Destructive and constructive feedback

Constructive feedback is obviously what we would aspire to be giving. It can help to solve problems and, by building trust, it can strengthen relationships. Being constructive can reduce stress (for both parties) and it will, therefore, help development. *Destructive* feedback simply makes things worse. It concentrates on attitudes, damages relationships, increases stress and hinders development.

Sometimes you may have a challenging post-observation conversation/review with a colleague who did not perform well – but who thinks he or she did. In such a conversation you may need to work hard to address issues you know to be weak. When you give feedback that is negatively critical:

- **Try to preface it with something positive.**
- **Be as specific as possible.**
- **Always check understanding.**
- **Ask whether he or she agrees or not.**
- **Ask him or her if he or she can think of anything he or she is going to do differently.**
- **Ask if he or she has ever heard anything similar about himself or herself before.**
- **Ask him or her to think or talk through the consequences of acting or not acting on the feedback given.**
- **Summarise.**

This is a challenging and much more difficult conversation to manage. It is a conversation that needs accurate and objective data to support your observations. However, it is still important to try to help the NQT, by skilful questioning, to realise there are some important issues to be tackled. Use such questions as:

- **You said you were pleased that... What specifically makes you say that?**
- **What did you notice about the way they entered and left the room?**
- **Was that what you expected?**
- **How do you think it could be improved?**
- **Do you think the children on the green table understood the task?**
- **How do you feel your questioning went?**

All these may be opening up areas for further discussion but you must have specific information to refer to. For example, you may have found out that the children on the green table hadn't a clue and just went through the motions of being busy! Alternatively, you may have recorded that every question asked was a closed one and no one on the right-hand side of the room was invited to respond.

In the extreme and most difficult situations, if all else fails, you will need to give *specific* feedback and to be very structured, perhaps using the guidance given in this chapter. This feedback must be recorded accurately, and there will almost certainly be some issues of teaching performance to be addressed through a structured approach to objective-setting.

Section Five

Helping your NQT to set objectives and to plan for his or her professional development

What is next? You have observed your NQT teach a few times, perhaps. You have had some really precise discussion about his or her work and you have, together, identified some issues that are important for your new colleague. This, of course, is where an induction tutor needs to be skilled in helping with the setting and achieving of the objectives for professional development.

The TTA guidance (1999, p. 24) is quite clear on this:

> Professional development objectives provide a strong sense of purpose and direction to those directly involved in induction. They help NQTs not only to meet the Induction Standards but also to look towards their longer term professional development once the Standards have been met. They also provide a basis for reviewing NQTs' progress, and enable NQTs and their induction tutors to identify both the aspects of the induction programme that are supporting improvement and the areas in which changes need to be made.

Objective-setting and continuing professional development

Professional development is not something we do *to* people. When senior colleagues make comments such as 'He needs developing' or 'We must develop her', there is perhaps a misunderstanding about the purpose of professional development. We are all responsible for our *own* professional development, and this includes NQTs. What schools and school leaders are responsible for, on the other hand, is providing the permitting circumstances, the learning culture where colleagues have the opportunities to grow professionally. So we do not set targets *for* an NQT, any more than we do *for* a pupil. We set them *with* an NQT. This involves discussion and collaboration and is more likely to result in ownership and successful outcomes.

Objective-setting means more than writing down an objective. It involves working through a process. First, let's think of some of the principles of objective-setting:

- **We need to be clear of the purposes and benefits of objective-setting.**
- **We must give attention to the process of identifying objectives.**
- **Overloading is dangerous, and so we must give thought to number and complexity.**
- **Objectives need to be precise, not ambiguous.**
- **We need to agree about what observable or measurable success will look like.**
- **Objectives should be challenging but realistic.**
- **Objectives must be accompanied by a mutually agreed action plan – however small.**

It seems that one of the classic management mistakes made by many organisations and individuals, from governments to headteachers, is to begin the development of any objective by starting in the wrong place. There are key words to address when embarking upon any development:

- *What* (am I/are we seeking to develop)?
- *Why* (is this important)?
- *How will we know* (when we are successful)?
- *How* (will we do it)?

The mistake is to go straight to the 'how?' We should begin with addressing 'what?' No doubt as a result of lesson observation, a particular aspect of teaching has been noted that requires further development. It may be an easy target to achieve within a short time, or it may be a much bigger issue that will be ongoing over the term or even longer. Next, we look at 'why?' What is the reason, the rationale for spending time on this? Is it really important and worth while? How does it fit? Having established that, we must be clear about what success will look like. *How will we know* when the objective has been achieved?

Only then do we begin on the process of planning the action. What we don't do is to leave an NQT floundering with some objective he or she desperately wants to achieve — but does not know how to go about it! There are several potential benefits when we use objective-setting as a development tool. Objective-setting *can*:

- **provide structured and supported professional growth for the NQT and others;**
- **build confidence and security by the recognition of successful achievement;**
- **support a school culture of collaboration;**
- **help to reduce individual stress by prioritising and helping to overcome problems;**
- **spread good practice;**
- **link individual and whole-school development;**
- **link with performance management.**

Helping your NQT to set objectives

Take time to consider the principles, purposes and benefits of objective-setting, as well as the need to comply with the induction arrangements. First, discuss with your new colleague those areas he or she feels to be strengths and those areas where he or she feels development and support are needed. This, of course, will change as the year progresses, but is likely to begin with the CEP. However, it is worth remembering that areas for development identified on the last school experience may not be priorities in the NQT's new school.

Having identified areas that may become objectives, agree on some priorities and work initially on one relatively easy target to test out the process (see later). Use the criteria suggested earlier to shape up the words of the objective. Once you have an objective, build it into a proposal, which will include the following:

- **Clarify precisely what the objective is and the purpose for achieving it.**

- **Agree on what success will look like.**

- **Agree on an action plan that includes who will do what, when this will happen and when progress will be reviewed.**

- **Record the agreed target and agree on who should see it. Then celebrate success.**

So far in our examples we have tended to focus mainly on teaching and learning issues. Experience shows us that the first attempts at report writing or parents' evenings are often a concern. Figure 17 is an example of how one induction tutor has worked with an NQT on a target relating to writing reports on pupil progress. In this example, the short time spent on the action planning can save a great deal of wasted time later. There are some obvious, but easily missed, steps that can be taken. With regard to *who* and *when*, the objective has a two-way accountability. The NQT has responsibilities and so do others – in this case, the induction tutor.

Early warnings of problems

Some teachers suggest that an NQT should be left to settle in before any structured monitoring and support are offered. This is not our view. Neither is a heavy-handed, intensive approach. Starting a new job is stressful, and a frequent but light touch will be appreciated. At this stage, support is more important than monitoring and assessment. However, within four weeks of starting, an NQT should have been observed teaching at least once. The experience of managing this (together with a month working with this colleague) will provide a range of indicators for the induction tutor, from planning to teaching, behaviour management and common sense. There may be some early warning bells about the competence and progress of your newly qualified colleague. These may relate to your impressions formed by your observations of how he or she behaves, what he or she says or contributes, his or her attendance, general disposition and uninvited observations from other colleagues. These need to be followed up. It is vital to arrive at the facts and not to rely on impression and hearsay. This may involve testing your skills of communication – listening, questioning and managing potentially difficult conversations.

Only when you are clear about the facts can you begin to take action. Within four weeks you will have observed one lesson and no doubt will have had several conversations. If you judge that there is an emerging problem, bring it out into the open in a sensitive, professional way and seek to address it with your new colleague. You will have to decide whether this needs to be communicated at this point to the co-ordinating member of the senior management team. However, it is important to keep a

Objective
To ensure my first set of written reports to parents are of high quality (due Christmas).

Purpose
1. To fulfil my professional responsibility.
2. To give useful feedback for parents and children.
3. To gain confidence in preparing for parents' evening.
4. To enhance the quality of in-school information on children.

How	Who	When	Review progress
Check school policy to clarify 1. agreed purpose/outcomes of reports for parents, pupils, teachers 2. what information to include/attitudes to reflect in reports.	NQT	This week	
Look at samples of school reports written by experienced teachers.	Mentor provides NQT to peruse	This week Next week	
Draft reports on 5 different pupils in class. Discuss these.	NQT NQT + induction tutor	By end of October By November 5th 4.00 pm	November 5th at review meeting
Write full set of reports. Discuss these and amend if necessary.	NQT NQT + induction tutor	By November 18th By November 23rd 4.00 pm	
Review whole process after parents' evening.	NQT NQT + induction tutor	By December 12th By December 16th	December 17th at review meeting

Evidence for success
- The reports themselves: do they meet school purposes and reflect good practice? (Discussions with mentor.)
- Feedback (informal) from parents (on parents' evening), children (in class review), colleagues.
- Personal review: level of satisfaction and confidence gained from the process.

Figure 17. The process of designing and achieving a focused action plan for an agreed objective.

record of your conversation and, if an outcome is a target together with the means of achieving it, all the better. Early concerns need to be treated carefully in a measured way. A sudden influx of massive support is likely to alarm the NQT. You have to judge what is appropriate.

Of course, we are dealing with one individual whose views may differ from our own. In the case of an NQT, perhaps the most challenging individual is the unconscious incompetent – the teacher who believes all is well when it is not. In such a situation you may reach a stage were you feel it appropriate to involve other colleagues who have a particular contribution to make.

In this unit you will find material to support you in the following areas:

SIGNPOST

- **developing your knowledge of the statutory framework for the** assessment of **the induction period;**

- **what to look for when assessing the standards;**

- **preparing and conducting the formal assessment meeting, including effective preparation of reports on the NQT's progress;**

- **using evidence in the evaluation process;**

- **approaching the assessment of an NQT who is at risk of not meeting the induction period requirements.**

Introduction and chapter overview

This chapter aims to provide you with key information and to support as you undertake the process of making a formal assessment of the induction period. It is divided into five sections. Section I identifies some key principles you may wish to bear in mind when you are making assessments of your newly qualified teachers (NQTs). This section underpins the remainder of the chapter and, as you read this, you will notice the principles are considered in the context of good practice in assessing induction.

Section 2 outlines in summary form the statutory requirements in relation to assessing the induction period and goes on to consider the responsibilities the school has in relation to fulfilling these. Section 3 explores the idea of the induction standards in more detail and makes more practical suggestions about what you may wish to look for when assessing the extent to which your NQT has achieved these. Section 4 focuses on the actual assessment meeting and considers issues of preparation, conduct and report writing. It also considers the role that evidence has to play in the whole process of assessing the induction period. Section 5 is concerned with strategies you may wish to use in relation to an NQT who is at risk of not meeting the requirements of the induction period.

Taken together, it is hoped these sections will be of direct practical relevance in supporting your work in this critical area of induction year mentoring.

Section One

Some key principles underpinning effective assessment of the induction period

It is important that, as induction tutor, you get the assessment of your NQT's induction period right. For the vast majority of NQTs their assessment will be unproblematic, but the stakes are high. Your NQT will have gone through a rigorous and demanding assessment process prior to the induction period. This will have involved the following:

- **Completion of a relevant degree.**

- **Detailed assessment against the standards for the award of Qualified Teacher Status (QTS) in both the practice of teaching and knowledge and understanding requirements.**

- **Successful completion of the range of national skills tests set by the Teacher Training Agency (TTA).**

If you put yourself in the position of your NQT, it is easy to see why the assessment of the induction year for some will be a process that generates a certain amount of anxiety. Should the NQT fail to meet the requirements of the induction period, it follows the opportunity to teach in maintained schools or non-maintained special schools is withdrawn. There are clearly key messages here for those involved in initial teacher training (ITT) to ensure that only those who are *clearly* able to teach and fulfil the QTS standards are awarded QTS in the first place.

A first principle, then, in assessing your NQT is to acknowledge that, for him or her, the 'stakes will be high'. Your assessment of his or her teaching matters greatly, particularly when you consider the consequences of failing and, more positively, the rigour of the assessment he or she should have experienced prior to the award of QTS. A consequence of this principle is that you will wish to conduct the assessment in a fair, accurate and compassionate way.

Secondly, you may have noticed the structure of the national assessment pro formas. This suggests the assessment of the induction period is relatively 'light touch', except when there is a risk of your NQT failing to meet the requirements. The pro forma is short and does not require a very detailed record of your assessment. It follows that the assessment of the induction period is not the same as the detailed assessment of what is required for the award of QTS in initial training. This may be an important point to bear in mind if you are involved in assessing trainees against the standards for QTS. The assessment processes in initial training and induction are similar but different.

Another underpinning principle is that your assessment must be valid. It must be an accurate reflection of the teaching abilities of your NQT. This means you will wish to ensure that your assessment is based on evidence from a number of different sources, including observation, the NQT's self-assessment, pupils' work and so forth.

It is also important that the assessment involves a number of different perspectives from relevant colleagues involved in the process, including those external to the school. If there is any risk of your NQT's failing to meet the requirements, this is, of course, essential.

In the vast majority of cases where the focus of assessment is the extent and *ways* in which NQTs have met the induction standards rather than any question of their not having fulfilled the requirements, the assessment process should be done *with* the NQT rather than *to* him or her. We think there is a subtle but important difference here between the assessment process in ITT and that in induction, which focuses on the relationship you will have with trainees and NQTs. You will appreciate that, when you are assessing your NQTs, you are assessing a qualified professional who has already met the threshold for that profession at the point of entry. This should and will create a different dynamic in your relationship with that person when compared with the trainee who has yet to meet the QTS threshold. Essentially, this dynamic will be concerned with a more equal status that will have implications particular to the conduct of the assessment. It is also relevant to mention here that the national report pro formas contain a section where the school has (quite rightly in our view) to record the support that has been afforded to the NQT. In addition, the NQT has a right of reply to whatever has been written about him or her.

A final principle is that the two major aspects of the induction period, support and monitoring and assessment, must be entwined and integrated. The assessment of your NQT's induction period cannot be valid unless the support is present to enable progress to be made and achievements to be achieved. There is, in this respect, a contrast between the old probationary year abolished by the then Education Secretary, Kenneth Clarke, in 1992, and the induction period implemented in 1999. The former focused very much on making judgements about individual progress and achievements with fairly minimal focus on any process of systematic individual professional development. The latter has sophisticated *linkage* of support and assessment and both of these are made explicit in the national arrangements for induction. We consider it to be a mistake to see that the old probationary year and the new induction year have similar frameworks and structures. They are, in essence, very different, and it may well be helpful if you approach the induction period without any preconceptions based on the old probationary year, if that is what you experienced. Induction is certainly not back to probation!

Some key principles underpinning assessment in the induction period

- For NQTs the stakes are high, given the rigour of assessment in initial training and the consequences of failure.
- Assessment of the induction period should normally be light touch.
- Assessment of the induction period should be valid.
- Assessment should be done with, not to, the NQT.
- Assessment and support/monitoring should be related.

For us, these principles underline the critical role of the induction tutor as 'gatekeeper to the profession'. Whether an NQT is allowed to enter the profession as a full member is largely in the hands of existing members of that profession. This has to be right because it involves a process of self-renewal, but it does carry with it a serious responsibility in regard to both the NQT as an individual and the profession in general.

Section Two

Assessing the induction year: the national requirements

DfEE Circular 0090/2000 (DfEE, 2000c) defines the main national requirements with regard to assessing the induction period. This section aims to summarise these requirements to provide you with an overview.

The most important events in the assessment process are the three assessment meetings. Where the NQT is working full time in a school with a standard three-term structure, the assessment meetings should take place at the end of each term and will normally involve you, your NQT and your headteacher or a head of department. Each assessment meeting should have a different purpose, using the different focuses of the induction period:

- **In the first term of the induction period, the focus should be on the extent to which your NQT is consistently meeting the standards for QTS against which he or she was assessed prior to qualification. It therefore follows that the assessment meeting should make an evidence-based summation judgement about whether your NQT has consistently met the QTS standards. This does not involve a detailed reassessment of the QTS standards but will focus on a broadly based consideration of these.**

- **During the second term of the induction period, the focus will change to whether your NQT is making progress towards the induction standards. These are considered in more detail in the next section but, as you can see, are fewer in number than the QTS standards. The assessment meeting will then need to consider whether satisfactory progress is being made towards the induction standards.**

- **The assessment meeting in the final term will essentially consist of an evidence-based judgement of whether your NQT has met all the requirements necessary for completing the induction period satisfactorily.**

If your NQT is not employed full time, it will be the case that the assessment meetings will be appropriately spaced out, but the circular states that the first assessment meeting should in any case occur at the end of the first term. In some cases NQTs will complete their induction period in a number of different schools and here it is important you maintain and retain good-quality records in relation to the whole assessment process.

Each assessment meeting must be evidence based and, whilst a range of evidence should be submitted, particular emphasis is placed on observations and the professional review meetings (where progress against individual objectives recorded in the

Career Entry Profile (CEP) is noted). Other sources of evidence will include the following:

- **Self-assessment undertaken by the NQT in relation to the QTS standards and/or the induction standards.**
- **The NQT's planning, evaluation and records of pupils' progress. This may include the results of national tests for pupils for which the NQT has direct and sustained responsibility.**
- **Information about how the NQT is liaising with others, including other colleagues and parents.**

The significant point here is to see that different parts of the evidence base have different importance. The observations and professional review meetings are seen as the main focus for the evidence to be used in the assessment meetings, whilst other elements are seen as less important and more peripheral to the whole process. It should also be the case that the assessment process is normally informed by *illustrative* evidence. It is not usual for each individual standard to be informed by separate evidence, although where a NQT is at risk of failing to meet the requirements of the induction period, then it follows that the evidence base will have to be more comprehensive.

At each assessment meeting you will need to complete the relevant part of a standard national assessment pro forma. The pro formas are reproduced in the Appendix so you can see its structure and framework. We have also partly completed the pro formas so you can get a sense of the recording process, which is fairly broadly based. You may wish to note that, at the time of writing, the national pro formas are under review.

There is a requirement for the completed pro forma to be sent by the headteacher to the 'appropriate body', normally within ten days of the meeting. The appropriate body for all LEA schools will almost always be the local education authority. Following the third assessment meeting, the assessment pro forma should be sent to the LEA, again within ten days. The LEA then has to make a decision about whether your NQT has completed the requirements of the induction period satisfactorily. The maximum time this should normally take is twenty working days. The LEA informs the school, the NQT and the General Teaching Council about the outcome of the assessment of the induction period. (The main features of the assessment process are shown in Figure 18.)

Avoiding possible pitfalls

There are a number of issues that, as assessor, you may wish to consider as you set up the assessment process for your NQT. Many of these issues are important, particularly in the event of the NQT challenging any elements of your assessment:

- **It is important you adopt a quasi-legalistic approach to your work as assessor. In particular, this means ensuring that 'the letter' of the process is followed. There**

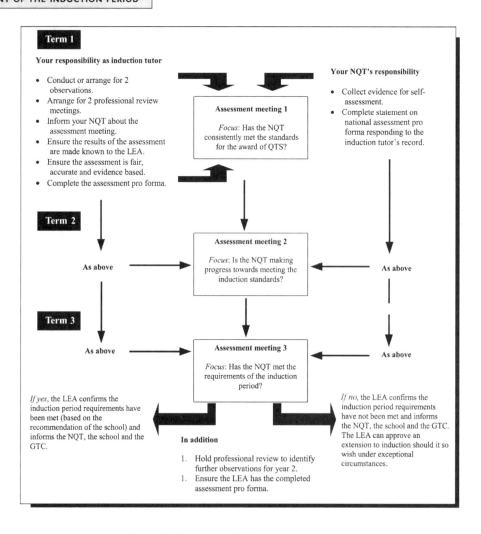

Figure 18. A summary of the assessment process.

should be three formal assessment meetings with each having the relevant specific focus. The **NQT** should be informed about when the assessment meeting is going to take place and should be given an appropriate time space for preparation. The evidence for the meeting should be clearly identifiable and related explicitly to the standards. The **NQT** should be offered the opportunity to contribute to the relevant section of the national assessment pro forma. Time gaps specified in the circular, especially in regard to the submission of pro formas, should be observed, and so forth. Observation of this framework will ensure that the assessment is conducted according to the **NQT's** entitlement.

- It is essential that early problems are recorded at the first assessment meeting. This will ensure that the **NQT** has a full opportunity to put matters right with proper support and monitoring from yourself. It will also make it much easier for you to decide, eventually and in very rare cases, that an **NQT** has failed to meet the induction year requirements. The basic point here is that, if there are difficulties, even these should be clearly specified.

- You should be clear about the distinction between the assessment meetings and the professional review meetings. The latter involve a structured review of progress towards professional objectives set as part of the process of your **NQT** completing the **CEP**, whereas the former involve focusing on the requirements for the induction period. This, by definition, will be much wider than the achievement of any one particular set of objectives.

- The assessment meeting should normally have an agenda so that all attending are clear about its purpose and focus. In the sample agenda shown in **Figure 19**, there is a systematic consideration of the standards against an evidence base.

Joanne Smith's assessment meeting: term 2 (4 March 2002)

Agenda

1. Establishing the key question: in what ways is Joanne making progress towards the induction standards?

2. Consideration of the planning, teaching and classroom management standards (key evidence base: observations carried out in January and February).

3. Consideration of the monitoring, assessment, recording, reporting and accountability standards (key evidence base: records of pupils' progress in mathematics).

4. Consideration of the other professional requirements standards (key evidence: Joanne's self-assessment).

5. Completing the assessment pro forma.

Figure 19. The assessment meeting: a sample agenda.

- If you feel (in very rare cases) that there is a danger of an **NQT** not meeting the requirements of the induction period, then we would like to emphasise the point we alluded to above. The evidence base for the assessment meeting is likely to be more wide ranging and comprehensive than in cases where the assessment is unproblematic. It will also be important for you to ensure that another colleague is present at the assessment meeting in order that there can be no doubt about the assessments being made. Normally, this would be a senior colleague, such as the headteacher in a primary school.

You may consider some of these points to be rather harsh and perhaps lacking in compassion. However, we believe that, to follow them, particularly in problematic cases, *is in both your interest and that of the NQT*. If there are difficulties it is right and fair that your NQT knows about this in a clear fashion, that this is depersonalised through the criteria of an appropriate evidence base, and that every support is put in place to ensure the NQT's practice is moved forward.

Assessing the standards: what to look for

This section will be particularly important if you have not had recent, direct experience of mentoring and assessing trainees and if you don't have current knowledge of

Section Three

the QTS standards. It has already been established that there are two sets of standards you will have to consider as you approach the assessment meetings. In the first term you will need to make a judgement concerning the extent to which your NQT has *consistently* met the QTS standards outlined in DfEE Circular 4/98 (DfEE, 1998). In the second two terms the focus will be on the induction standards. Let us consider the major differences between these two sets of standards. Below is a selection of the QTS standards, which is followed by the induction standards in their entirety.

1. The QTS standards are more numerous and detailed than the induction standards. This will have implications for how they are used in assessment.

2. There are four sections in the standards for the award of QTS:
    (a) subject knowledge and understanding (section A);

A sample of the standards for the award of QTS
(from Section B, 'Planning, teaching and class management')

a. plan their teaching to achieve progression in pupils' learning through:

   (i)   identifying clear teaching objectives and content, appropriate to the subject matter and the pupils being taught, and specifying how these will be taught and addressed;
   (ii) setting tasks for whole class, individual and group work, including homework, which challenge pupils and ensure high levels of pupil interest;
   (iii) setting appropriate and demanding expectations for pupils' learning, motivation and presentation of work;
   (iv) setting clear targets for pupils' learning, building on prior attainment, and ensuring that pupils are aware of the substance and purpose of what they are asked to do;
   (v)   identifying pupils who:

   * have special educational needs, including specific learning difficulties;
   * are very able;
   * are not yet fluent in English;

   and knowing where to get help in order to give positive and targeted support;

b. provide clear structures for lessons, and for sequences of lessons, in the short, medium and longer term, which maintain pace, motivation and challenge for pupils;

c. make effective use of assessment information on pupils' attainment and progress in their teaching and in planning future lessons and sequences of lessons;

d. plan opportunities to contribute to pupils' personal, spiritual, moral, social and cultural development;

e. where applicable, ensure coverage of the relevant examination syllabuses and National Curriculum programmes of study.

The induction standards (DfEE, 2000c)

To meet the Induction Standards, the NQT should demonstrate that he or she:

Planning, Teaching and Class Management

a. sets clear targets for improvement of pupils' achievement, monitors pupils' progress towards those targets and uses appropriate teaching strategies in the light of this, including, where appropriate, in relation to literacy, numeracy and other school targets;

b. plans effectively to ensure that pupils have the opportunity to meet their potential, notwithstanding differences of race and gender, and taking account of the needs of pupils who are:
   - underachieving;
   - very able;
   - not yet fluent in English;

   making use of relevant information and specialist help where available;

c. secures a good standard of pupil behaviour in the classroom through establishing appropriate rules and high expectations of discipline which pupils respect, acting to pre-empt and deal with inappropriate behaviour in the context of the behaviour policy of the school;

d. plans effectively, where applicable, to meet the needs of pupils with Special Educational Needs and, in collaboration with the SENCO, makes an appropriate contribution to the preparation, implementation , monitoring and review of Individual Education Plans;

e. takes account of ethnic and cultural diversity to enrich the curriculum and raise achievement.

Monitoring, Assessment, Recording, Reporting and Accountability

f. recognises the level that a pupil is achieving and makes accurate assessments, independently, against attainment targets, where applicable, and performance levels associated with other tests or qualifications relevant to the subject(s) or phase(s) taught;

g. liaises effectively with pupils' parents/carers through informative oral and written reports on pupils' progress and achievements, discussing appropriate targets, and encouraging them to support their children's learning, behaviour and progress.

Other Professional Requirements

h. where applicable, deploys support staff and other adults effectively in the classroom, involving them, where appropriate, in the planning and management of pupils' learning;
i. takes responsibility for implementing school policies and practices, including those dealing with bullying and racial harassment;
j. takes responsibility for their own professional development, setting objectives for improvements, and taking action to keep up-to-date with research and developments in pedagogy and in the subject(s) they teach.

National Tests in Numeracy

k. to complete induction successfully an NQT trained in England, qualifying on or after 1 May 2000 and before May 2001, must have passed the national test for teacher training candidates in numeracy, before the completion of the induction period. Candidates have five opportunities to pass the test.*

*The Secretary of State proposed to determine this standard under the Education (Induction Arrangements for School Teachers) (Amendment No 2) (England) Regulations 2000 which have been made and, subject to parliamentary approval, came into force on 25 May 2000. (*All trainees gaining QTS after May 2001 will already have passed TTA skills tests in numeracy and literacy.*)

(b) planning, teaching and classroom management (section B);

(c) monitoring, assessment, recording, reporting and accountability (section C);

(d) other professional requirements (section D).

There are three sections in the induction standards:

(a) planning, teaching and classroom management;

(b) monitoring, assessment, recording, reporting and accountability;

(c) other professional requirements.

3. Some of the QTS standards make reference to specific pieces of knowledge, particularly in sections A and D: knowledge and understanding and other professional requirements.

4. The induction standards do not contain a section on subject knowledge and understanding. There is, here, an implication that this is assessed prior to the award of QTS and is hence taken as acquired in the induction period. Moreover, the national pro forma for recording the assessment of your NQT does not contain a section on subject knowledge and understanding for term I when you are assessing the consistent meeting of the QTS standards. Should you feel there are any further significant gaps in subject knowledge, these could be recorded in the section of the pro forma that focuses on planning, teaching and classroom management. Figure 3 in the standards provides a case study of how an induction tutor dealt with a primary NQT who had some significant gaps in her science subject knowledge.

5. The QTS standards contain specific sections for trainees teaching in the early years.

6. Because the QTS standards are so numerous, it will be important for these to be clustered so that the assessments you are making are reasonable and achievable and in accordance with the principle of light-touch assessment.

7. Induction standards progress from the QTS standards in the sense that many go beyond expected characteristics displayed at the point of the QTS being awarded. There is an enhanced expectation of independence in professional behaviour related to school, local and national policies.

Assessing the consistent meeting of the QTS and induction standards

Grouping NQT standards around a series of clusters is essential if their assessment is to be realistic. This is, in any case, in tune with Circular 4/98 (DfEE, 1998, p. 8):

Each standard will not require a separate assessment occasion. Groups of standards are closely linked and are designed so that they can be assessed together. While providers must be confident that all the standards have been met before they make a final decision to recommend the award of QTS, this should not require a mechanistic, tick-list approach or entail each standard being supported by its own evidence base. To reflect the complexity of the teaching process being assessed, providers are likely to make over-arching judgements, taking account of evidence from the wide range of sources available to them across partnerships. This should enable providers, if necessary, to explain and justify their overall decision, including to trainees and other colleagues. The standards might also be used near the end of training to identify any particular areas where they may be unclear about a trainee's knowledge, understanding and skills, to help focus the provider's observations of, discussions with, and requirements of trainees, so that a confident decision can be made.

In *Succeeding in the Induction Year* (Simco, 2000), a series of questions relating to both sets of induction standards was developed for NQTs to consider in any self-assessment. Here these questions are adapted for your use as the induction tutor (see Figure 20). There are two columns, the first of which relates to the QTS standards. We suggest you may wish to use these questions as you consider the extent to which your NQT has met the relevant standards. However, in some cases, particularly where there is any doubt about whether an NQT has met the standards, it will be necessary for assessment to be based on the exact words of the standards. In the figure, each set of questions is coded against the student's so you can easily identify the standards.

You may wish to use the question grids in a number of ways to support the process of assessing your NQT against the national criteria:

- **Scan the relevant column and identify two or three questions you may wish to use as key focuses in the assessment meeting.**

- **Ask your NQT to self-assess against the questions, hence identifying strengths and areas for professional development.**

- **Ascertain the nature of progression between the standards for the award of QTS and the induction standards, and be explicit about this in your assessment meeting.**

- **Use the general strategy of posing a series of questions when looking in more detail at an individual standard, particularly when there is doubt whether this has been fully achieved.**

- **Structure the agenda for the assessment meeting using selected key questions.**

- **Use the language of the key questions when you write the report; they summarise the national requirements for induction.**

The assessment meetings and the use of evidence

Section Four

In section 2 some notion of the assessment meeting was introduced as a central part of the statutory induction arrangements. You will recall that your obligation is to ensure there are three assessment meetings carried out in the induction year, focused variously on the extent to which the NQT is consistently achieving the QTS

Consistently meeting the QTS standards?	Meeting the induction standards?
Planning, Teaching and Class Management	

Planning

To what extent:

- Does your NQT's planning demonstrate his or her awareness of progression in pupils' learning?
- Does your NQT's planning (short, medium, long term) set clear objectives for learning?
- Is your planning appropriate to the age group being taught?
- Does your planning demonstrate your NQT has high expectations for *all* pupils' learning?
- Does your NQT's planning show clear structures for lessons?
- Is your NQT's planning related to examination syllabuses/programmes of study?
- Does planning make effective use of previous assessments on pupils and take account of their personal, spiritual, moral, social and cultural development?

Teaching

- Does your NQT's teaching approaches encourage pupils' sustained engagement with this work?
- Are teaching approaches related to pupils and subject matter?
- Is teaching and intervention effective in whole-class, group and individual contexts?
- Are lessons well structured?
- Are questioning, explanation and lesson presentation clear?

Meeting the induction standards?

To what extent:

- Does your NQT understand the place of target-setting in raising pupil achievement? And plans accordingly? **(2(a))**
- Is there evidence that school targets are taken into account when setting targets for pupils? **(2(a))**
- Does your NQT's planning differentiate appropriately such that there is provision for all pupils to achieve their potential? **(2(b))**
- Does your NQT's planning use resources which reflect cultural diversity? **(2(e))**
- Is there evidence of appropriate intervention in learning to ensure that targets are met? **(2(a))**

Figure 20. Key questions to use when assessing the induction period.

- Is the pace of teaching appropriate?
- Are pupils listened to and are misconceptions identified and dealt with appropriately?
- Are there opportunities for pupils to consolidate this learning?
- Is there an appropriate selection of resources for learning, including textbooks and ICT materials?
- Are learning opportunities explicit in relation to numeracy, literacy and ICT and in personal, spiritual, social and cultural development?
- Are learning opportunities related to real and work-related examples?
- Does your NQT have familiarity with the special educational needs code of practice?
- Are records kept and individual education plans implemented for pupils at stage two of the code and above with guidance from one experienced teacher?

Class management

- Does your NQT have high expectations of pupils' behaviour?
- Is there a sustained good standard of discipline and a safe working environment?

If your NQT is in an early year's setting

- Does he or she manage other adults in the classroom and use play as a vehicle for learning?
- Are learning opportunities provided that relate to the early learning goals, including the foundations for literacy and numeracy?
- Do learning opportunities encourage pupils to think about their learning, concentrate and work towards independence?

- Is differentiation apparent in your NQT's teaching? (2(b))
- Does your NQT's teaching use resources which reflect cultural diversity? (2(e))
- Does your NQT take his or her share of the responsibility for developing and implementing IEPs in an increasingly independent fashion? (2(d))

- Is there evidence that inappropriate behaviour is *anticipated* and effectively deflected? (2(c))
- Does your NQT know of and use the school behaviour policy effectively? (2(c))

Figure 20 (continued). Key questions to use when assessing the induction period.

and induction standards. You will also recall these meetings should be approached in a quasi-legalistic (but still compassionate!) manner. The purpose of this section is to look a little closer at these meetings and to provide you with some material to consider as you begin to set these up.

An example will provide us with a context in which to consider these issues:

Keith was working in the reception unit of a suburban primary school in the south of England. He had 24 children in his class and worked closely with Kym, the nursery nurse. His mentor was Rachel, who was head of the foundation key stage unit, which included both reception classes and the large nursery attached to the school. During the early part of the first term of the induction year, Keith had been observed by his induction tutor and had also had ample opportunity to observe in other classes in order to work towards the objectives specified in his CEP. One of these related to him understanding progression from nursery to reception and here he had already had a series of meetings with the nursery teacher, each one focused on a different area of the Early Learning Goals (ELGs). In mid-November of his first term, Rachel wanted to set up the assessment meeting. She wanted to discuss this process at one of the regular tutorials that were held on a weekly basis. At this meeting the agenda for the assessment meeting was agreed, and it was also agreed what evidence would be cited in relation to each area of the standards. The purpose of this provisional meeting was to be reassuring and to ensure Keith had the opportunity to prepare properly for the assessment meeting. For section B of the QTS standards, the assessment meeting would focus on the two observations that would have occurred by then, together with a sample of Keith's planning. For section C of the QTS standards, Keith would bring along his records of baseline assessment, which would have been completed at the beginning of the term, whilst for section D the focus would be a short report from Kym, the nursery nurse, which considered the extent to which Keith had deployed her effectively within the unit and had built up a good-quality professional working relationship. At the provisional meeting it was also agreed Keith would bring along a broadly based self-assessment containing information about how he had consistently met the QTS standards. The assessment meeting was scheduled for the penultimate week of the autumn term, and it was agreed Keith, Rachel and the headteacher would be present. The meeting lasted about 30 minutes and was very focused. It took place in Keith's classroom. Each section of the standards was considered in turn, with evidence being presented and Keith making comments about his achievements in the area. The specific piece of evidence for each standards area was considered first and then there was a brief wider discussion in relation to the section as a whole. Rachel completed the assessment pro forma at the end of the meeting and this was then passed to Keith, who added his comments prior to the form being sent off to the recommending body, in this case the local education authority.

It may be helpful now to analyse this case study so certain key issues can be identified. It is hoped you may find these useful as you set up assessment meetings, whether they be in reception or elsewhere within primary, middle or secondary contexts:

- **The first point to note is that the assessment meeting was properly planned for. The provisional meeting occurred in the context of a regular tutorial and thus dispensed with an extra meeting.**

- At this provisional meeting, care was taken to minimise the bureaucratic burden, in the sense that the evidence base required was very specific and fairly minimal. It was also the case that, in each area of the standards, the evidence base was centred on information that was readily available anyway; it didn't demand the collection of extensive further evidence.

- A range of different types of evidence was required, which included assessment of children's attainments carried out by Keith, observations of teaching, self-assessment and the short report from Kym. Other evidence could include an assessment of planning and the extent to which objectives recorded in section C of the CEP had been fulfilled, although it is important to note here that the completion of the CEP is not the same as meeting the standards for the induction period.

- The self-assessment aspect is particularly worthwhile for at least two reasons. First, it links with preparation for performance management where teacher self-assessment is a central tool. Secondly, it ensures the NQT is included in the assessment process. It provides an indication the assessment is done with, not to, the NQT.

- While there are no statutory requirements in this area, we think it makes good sense for you as induction tutor to involve at least one other person in the assessment meeting. It is a formal assessment meeting and the presence of a (preferably senior) person other than yourself and the NQT will ensure the assessment being made is valid.

- During the assessment meeting, specific evidence was cited for various of the standards, which was then used as a basis for a brief, broadly based discussion about other areas of the standards. In this way the discussion had a specific focus but also covered the gist of each of the areas of the standards.

- You will have noticed that, in the example above, the assessment meeting took place in Keith's classroom. This was quite deliberate as it gave Keith the message the assessment was being done with him, not to him. The location of the assessment meeting was on his own territory. Had Keith been 'summoned' to the headteacher's office or even Rachel's classroom, subtle messages would have been given about the style of the meeting as well as the notion that it was being 'done to' Keith.

- Linked to this it was also apparent the style of the meeting was very inclusive. When a summative assessment meeting is being conducted, it is very easy to be exclusive in as much as a judgement is delivered to the NQT, who receives it. In the case study, the NQT was fully involved in the discussion and the self-assessment that had been undertaken formed an important part of this discussion.

- Finally, you will have noticed in the case study that the formal assessment pro forma was completed directly after the meeting and handed to Keith for his own comment prior to being sent to the LEA. Again this is important. You will have noted that, at the beginning of this chapter, it was stated that the stakes are high for NQTs. They will have already been through a rigorous assessment for the award of QTS and are aware of the consequences of failing to meet all the requirements of the induction year. It is only right and proper that the assessment of the induction year is carried out with due regard for the pressures and degree of anxiety the NQT will almost inevitably feel.

Section Five

Dealing with an NQT who is at risk of not meeting the requirements of the induction period

Dealing with NQTs who are in a potentially failing position brings with it a number of particular responsibilities for you as induction tutor which go beyond the 'normal' requirements. However, the TTA is very clear in its anticipation that the number of NQTs who will fail the induction period in any one year will be relatively low. The following quotation comes from the national guidelines for induction published by the TTA: 'It is anticipated that the vast majority of NQTs will have a successful induction and the form used to make the recommendation requires little more than a "signing off" by the headteacher and the signature of the NQT' (TTA, 1999, p. 30). However, of course, it is the case that if you are dealing with an NQT who is at risk of failing to meet the requirements, it is perhaps of little comfort to know you are one of very few!

The formal position on NQTs who are making unsatisfactory progress is contained in paragraphs 74–84 and 88–93 of Circular 0090/2000, *The Induction Period for Newly Qualified Teachers* (DfEE, 2000c). This can be summarised as follows:

- **It is the responsibility of the headteacher to ensure there are procedures in school that will lead to the early detection of an NQT who is experiencing professional difficulties that may lead to a failure to meet the induction year requirements.**

- **Reports sent to the appropriate body should contain additional details relating to identified weaknesses, an action plan (including the identification of support for the NQT) and a description of the evidence base that will be used to make a summative judgement. Reports should also make it quite clear the NQT is at risk of failing to meet the requirements of the induction period.**

- **The headteacher and the appropriate body (normally the LEA) should assure themselves that the assessment the NQT is at risk is valid, and in particular the headteacher should observe the NQT teaching.**

- **The headteacher also has a responsibility to inform the NQT in writing of the consequences of failing to meet the requirements of the induction period and should provide a detailed indication of the steps the NQT needs to take in order to improve his or her position and the support that will be put in place in order to achieve this. The NQT has an obligation to inform the LEA if he or she feels the support offered is any sense inadequate.**

- **The role of the induction tutor is not specified clearly in the circular, but if the NQT is deemed to be at risk, the implication is that in your role you will be particularly active in the support and monitoring aspect. The formal assessment** element will be transferred in many cases to the headteacher in combination with **LEA** officers.

- If the recommendation from the school is that the **NQT** fails the induction period requirements, the national pro forma should be completed and sent to the **LEA**, containing the recommendation of fail. It is the appropriate body who makes the decision and this should in turn be transmitted to the **NQT**. The **NQT** can make an appeal to the appeals body, who can allow the appeal, dismiss the appeal or extend the induction period.

- Should the fail be confirmed, there are significant employment consequences for the **NQT**, who is no longer eligible to be employed as a teacher in a maintained school or non-maintained special school.

In all schools where there are early signs the NQT is likely not to satisfy the induction year requirements, the headteacher will be substantially involved to the extent that, as induction tutor, your responsibility would be limited. Indeed, in some schools, the induction tutor would have no direct involvement in the assessment meeting. There are, however, normally a number of key elements to your response. In situations where there are potentially failing NQTs, you need to be very clear about the nature of your responsibility: it is not your responsibililty to ensure that the NQT passes, because the progress that is made is (given appropriate support) the responsibility of the NQT; instead, your responsibility centres on the provision of that support. In the first place this needs effective diagnosis, and when you first realise there is a problem, you will involve a senior colleague at an early stage. You then have a responsibility, in consultation with others, to put in place professional objectives which the NQT can progress towards in a way that can be measured. It is therefore particularly important that the targets are precise, the actions clear and that the environment in which this is taken forward with the NQT is supportive. It may well be that you negotiate to find some additional non-contact time so the NQT can observe good practice. You also need to note that the mere meeting of the professional objectives does not in itself guarantee that the NQT's situation has been transformed, because these are not the same thing as the QTS or induction standards. Beyond this, your main responsibility will be to inform the headteacher about progress being made, but your place in the formal assessment process will be diminished as this will become more the domain of the headteacher and the LEA inspector/adviser. We believe that an important principle in all this is early intervention. It is a question of professional judgement, but the worst thing to happen is that the failure emerges late in term three of the induction period. If this happens, then in an appeal the NQT would have strong grounds, as the argument that he or she did not have the opportunity to address his or her weaknesses would be overwhelming.

One of the reasons why we think it is important to see this issue in terms of carefully defined responsibilities is that the stakes for the NQT are very high. If you play a part in failing the NQT, you know that the consequences for him or her will be serious and far reaching, particularly after having trained for four years to gain his or her QTS. Clearly, there is a danger of your professional judgement being clouded by this realisation. Teachers *are* human beings! However, we feel that by fulfilling your responsibilities to provide an appropriate level of support and by acknowledging that the NQT has a responsibility to respond, you will be in a stronger position to contribute to the assessment process in a clear and objective way. It will also help if the NQT has access to informal emotional/social support, perhaps from a teacher who is not involved in the assessment process in any way. The bottom line is that, as induction tutor, you are one of a number of gatekeepers to the profession. If after early diagnosis, support and intervention there is no real progress, you have to ask whether you wish this person to be exposed to generations of pupils. Is this in his/her or the pupils' best interests?

What follows are the real stories of five induction tutors and their various experiences of managing the induction year and working with their newly qualified teacher. You will find case studies from primary, secondary and special schools, and we hope you will find them enlightening and thought-provoking.

Kate (secondary, foreign languages)

Story 1

'In this large school, continuing professional development has a high profile and we frequently have a number of newly qualified teachers [NQTs]. A member of the SMT [senior management team] co-ordinates induction and, knowing my interest, invited me to take some responsibility in this area. When I hear what happens to some NQTs it makes me weep and I've always thought about this work on the basis of how I'd like to be treated. Today, new teachers are more aware of what should happen, especially with regard to the new national arrangements. With hindsight, I certainly wouldn't have liked to have been an induction tutor without the full picture provided by the LEA training I received.

'Being an induction tutor this year has made me a better head of faculty because it has improved my people management. It is not very easy to combine supporting, on the one hand, and challenging on the other. My confidence has grown and this has renewed my interest and impetus. We all need to extend our skills and this work is compatible and complimentary to my main role. I am concerned we get good people into the profession and we need to give them good support.

'As an induction tutor it is a real bonus if you are involved in the selection process. I was involved in the shortlisting, interview and lesson observation and I had a key involvement in the decision to appoint.

'I remember our first meeting. It was GCSE results day. I felt it important at this stage for Charles to know what to do on the first day of term with his new classes. I talked through each class and we discussed what he could do in that first lesson. We also talked about his difficulty in finding accommodation and I helped him to find a flat. The day before term started, we met again and Charles spent the day familiarising himself with his room, resources and meeting departmental colleagues.

'It wasn't until our first formal meeting in early September that we looked at his Career Entry Profile [CEP]. I didn't find the vague comments very useful. There was no flavour about what sort of teacher he was. I already knew he planned well from the lesson I observed on interview, and it was also clear he was able to develop good relationships with the students.

'With regard to Charles's programme of support, at present suggestions still tend to come from me and I find it difficult to get him to come up with ideas. During the autumn, understandably, he didn't want to go out of school. However, this term there is a GCSE course and a national conference, which he is looking forward to attending. Charles receives three extra non-teaching periods a week for his reduced timetable but sometimes he might get used for cover. At the moment, we are looking at what is expected in a report for parents on a student's progress.

'An important area of development for me has been the way I manage the process of classroom observation. I've really moved forward in this and am much more thorough in the preparation stage before an observation. We agreed that, for the first observation, I'd come to a lesson where no one else had taught a modern foreign language to his class before. Bad habits allowed by others can develop. We focused by agreement on the use of the target language. When I observe, it's primarily to give support, advice and encouragement, but you are always assessing.

'When we review lesson observations together, we agreed that Charles would bring his own review to our conversation. I had to work hard to keep Charles from being too self-critical because there was a great deal of good practice in his teaching.

'Charles has also been observed by senior managers – they visit without negotiation. There is no focus and the purpose is for checking up and for assessment.

'I'm not present at the actual assessment meeting. It is run by the deputy and head. However, in preparation for this meeting, I worked with Charles to ensure he had a portfolio of evidence. This included examples of curriculum materials he had produced, reports he had written, exercise books, test results, lesson observation reviews and objectives and their progress.

'My work as an induction tutor has informed my other work, especially in performance management. The work I undertake on classroom observation and review is directly transferable and I feel I am much better at doing and saying difficult things in a supportive way, without causing offence. We tread a very fine line sometimes!'

Commentary

Kate is a head of faculty in a large high school where a deputy head has responsibility for providing leadership and co-ordination for continuing professional development, which has high priority and is well managed.

Kate was very motivated to undertake this work, and the school sensibly included her from the outset in the selection procedure because it was felt this was important for her own professional development, but also that it would be helpful in her future relationship with the NQT if she was party to his appointment.

From the outset, Kate was quick to focus her energies on issues relating to learning and teaching, although she did not find the comments on the CEP useful. Initial discussion focused immediately on the classroom and, for Kate, the management of the process of classroom observation was a key area, providing a vehicle for support, challenge and information to go towards assessment.

An important spin-off from this work for Kate is that it informs her other work as a head of faculty, and especially with regard to performance management and the development of her own interpersonal skills. Clearly, Kate's reflective comments tell us that there are several important outcomes for her.

Points to ponder

- Being involved in the selection procedure was seen to be important and helped along the relationship between the induction tutor and **NQT**.

- Being an induction tutor can provide opportunities to develop a range of interpersonal skills.

- Managing the process of classroom observation is demanding if it is to be well done, and this involves careful preparation and well managed review as well as observation.

- Striking a balance between support and challenge is important and not always easy.

- The work of an induction tutor links well with the responsibilities of a team leader in performance management, and it is inappropriate to see all the jobs of promoted postholders as discrete entities. The fact they overlap is transparent.

Joe (primary)   Story 2

'Back in July I felt quite apprehensive because it was a new challenge. Then the local HE [higher education] institution asked us to take some ITT [initial teacher training] students. The head asked me to take on responsibility for both these areas and, although at the time I didn't know what was involved, it was nice to be asked. We hadn't had an NQT or a student for five years. My school supported my training to undertake this work and I was fortunate to attend two training courses – one from the HE institution and one from the LEA. I then began to realise how much work was involved but because I wanted to do it and because it is about someone's professional development, you want to get it right.

'I saw this work as an opportunity to gain more management experience and I am fortunate in that I have a head who has allowed me to get on with the job, whilst showing an interest too. Next year we will have another NQT so this year's experience is important. Also, you don't get much help in your second year and so I intend that we extend the support beyond the first year. From my point of view, I am gaining valuable experience of observation, reviewing and running meetings. All this links well with performance management (I am a team leader) so I'm getting double the experience!

'Before I was trained as an induction tutor, I was blind to any problems. One thing I felt strongly about, following my training, was that I needed to go public about this work with the rest of the staff who were not aware of what was required of an induction tutor or an NQT. The NQT has to ask for things, and people need to understand what and why. The head agreed we would use part of a staff meeting for this, as a result of which everyone understands broadly what is required. However, one thing I want to do is to produce a school handbook, especially for the NQT, so that next year we don't need to start all over again.

'We first met during the summer holidays and we devoted this meeting to what Clare was going to teach and to see how this fitted in with the schemes of work. So we started off with planning for teaching. In September, we looked at what resources were available. At this stage, I had not been trained and I didn't really understand the role. However, we looked at Clare's CEP, talked about her background and what she saw as her key priorities and some ways of addressing these, especially in the 10% non-teaching time. This was a useful process and Clare was surprised at how seriously I was taking the CEP because it had been given little status at her training institution. It is easy to pick out the link between what she had written in section B – her areas for development – and the objective we agreed to work on in section C.

'In support of putting these objectives in the autumn term, Clare wanted to observe some experienced colleagues, especially teaching art and maths. At first, there was a problem with her allocated 10% non-teaching time because it was always on a Thursday morning. We overcame this with a more flexible approach to releasing her and also by accommodating staff who sometimes rearranged their lessons in order to help her. Once people understand the benefits, its interesting to see how helpful they can be.

'Clare is a very able NQT and it is important to be mindful of this. I have heard that, sometimes, an able NQT is perceived not to need the attention and opportunity because they are able! This seems to misunderstand what it is all about. After all, we cater for the able in our classrooms, so why not for the able NQT? During these first two terms, I have arranged for Clare (or rather she has arranged for herself) to observe six lessons – one in another school. Clare has been good at taking the initiative and, for example, wrote to all staff asking for an example of literacy work and levels of attainment to support one of her own objectives. During the spring term we looked specifically at the induction standards – they are useful but when you start to unpick them, they open up an amazing amount.

'On reflection, I feel much more confident about the role, especially as an observer in the classroom. I know what to do and what to look for, I do feel confident about knowing what is expected of me and I can now see how the structure all fits together. Time has been an issue, and always will be. However, I'm one of those people who likes to see the job through – but it is a lot to expect on top of all the other work. For example, we don't have a handbook, but I will still do it because I think it's worthwhile and important. One thing I've noticed is that there is a lot of transferability of skills and work to performance management and being a team leader and being a member of the SMT.

'Support for me has been excellent. The school allowed me time for training and staff meeting time to inform colleagues. I spent more time with Clare during the autumn term, when we had daily meetings. Additionally, observation, reviews and review meetings and an assessment meeting have taken up about 17 hours during the autumn and spring terms.

'One thing we can improve on is our management of the assessment meeting. It was not clear who was leading, me or the head. I also felt Clare was overworking – she was doing too much and I felt I couldn't stop her! I felt rather powerless. Also, I felt uncomfortable having to mediate between Clare and two other colleagues. In one instance, there was a colleague whose ways of working, standards and procedures were not a good exemplar for Clare. I needed to alert her to this. Another colleague proved at first to be inflexible over accommodating a lesson observation. The second of these I resolved, the first proved much more difficult.

'Finally, what is really important is the impact of all this work for Clare. Her feedback to me is very positive about what our school is doing to support her in this, all-important first year, and that's what counts. She is happy, gaining in competence and confidence and feels valued in a supportive environment where she can learn from her more experienced colleagues but is also recognised as a colleague who has much to offer.'

Commentary

Joe teaches in a large primary school and his headteacher recognised Joe was ready to take on responsibility for developing the school's provision since it was several years ago there had been an NQT in the school. To support Joe, the head ensured he had access to some comprehensive training to prepare him for this work, which will continue into the following year.

Once Joe understood the scope of the provision a school should make for induction, both he and the head wanted to ensure the whole staff understood what was required and that they all had a useful part to play. In order to facilitate this and give status to the work, the head ensured Joe was given air time at a staff meeting to bring his colleagues up to date with the latest arrangements and to highlight the potential benefits of effective induction to the school.

There has always been the issue in education that, so often, we provide training and support to colleagues only after they have begun to undertake a job. Joe made the point that it would have been easier if he could have begun training for the role of induction tutor before meeting his NQT! However, better late than never!

Joe started with Clare's CEP and gave it real status, which interestingly did not match the emphasis placed on this at her training institution. They both found this a useful point at which to start.

The culture of this school is clearly one where colleagues are prepared to collaborate and accommodate each other, as illustrated in the use of the 10% reduced timetable.

Points to ponder

- **A supportive headteacher, who made it possible for Joe to be prepared to undertake the role and also ensured the whole staff knew about the school's responsibilities in providing effective induction.**

- **All staff can be involved. They are the biggest resource the school has and this needs harnessing.**

- **Giving status to the CEP can promote valuable discussion, even when it has been used poorly.**

- **Approaching the 10% non-teaching time with creativity and imagination can ensure the best use is made of the time.**

- **Able NQTs should not be penalised for being able by being given fewer opportunities or less time.**

Story 3   Simon (primary)

'When our deputy head moved on to another school I asked to take on the induction work because I felt I was the right person to do this job. At the time, we didn't know whether we would have an NQT but, once we knew, I felt really pleased and privileged to be allowed to do this. I felt I must be doing something right! And then some self-doubt began to set in – would I be able to live up to our deputy's standard? Could I do that? I began to worry I might fall flat on my face. I enrolled on a course of training for induction tutors and, after the first day, my confidence returned, once I was clear what the job required.

'Unfortunately, I wasn't involved in the selection process and so the first time I met David was when I was introduced in the staffroom as his induction tutor. At our first proper meeting we looked at the Career Entry Profile and, quite frankly, what had been included in parts A and B was of little use and, whilst classroom management was indicated as a strength, by the end of the third day it was clear there was a lot of work to do.

'As the autumn term progressed, David didn't! He found it hard to relate to the children and had a lot of challenging behaviour from the most able and the children with learning difficulties in his class of 33. I felt so sorry for him. He was planning meticulously but it just wasn't happening for him. We were meeting two or three lunchtimes a week and an evening, because he just wasn't coping. He found the school a culture shock after his teaching practice schools. I felt I was no longer giving my own class 100% of my attention. Staff started coming up to me and saying, for example, "Just a quick word, Simon – David is having problems with…". In fact David was by now overwhelmed with advice from well meaning colleagues. He flitted from me to others and was trying out too many strategies all at once. The children didn't know whether they were coming or going – they became confused – they needed consistency and routine.

'For me, this was the lowest point of the year. We had a newly trained, well qualified teacher on the brink of throwing in the towel! I felt as though I was letting him down. However, one of my senior colleagues kept coming back and telling me I was doing a good job and that by focusing on some small steps, things would improve.

'Actually, when I look back, there are some school procedural things that weren't in place. Although I was given this responsibility, the staff were not informed by senior management. Furthermore, I was the only person in the school who actually had a clear grasp of what the induction year in 2001 really meant. My other colleagues were ignorant and saw, for example, the 10% extra time for the NQT in a rather negative way. I was told there was an induction policy in school, but have never been able to find it. I wish there had been one in place in September. It is different from having ITT students – they [NQTs] have to be treated differently. Apart from being granted the job, I do not feel the appropriate conditions existed for me to do the job. So, it has been down to me.

'We have sharpened the focus on classroom management and looked at practical strategies to help David to improve his practice. This has included working on differentiated materials, identifying particular children and their behaviours, and providing opportunities to observe experienced colleagues with a focus on subject and behaviour management. There was a suggestion from senior management for someone to take his class to demonstrate 'discipline in action'. I fought off this suggestion on the grounds it could have severely damaged David's self-esteem. David's voice was also hampering the climate in his classroom and we worked on modifications to volume, tone and expression.

'The outcome of our combined efforts is that David is progressing. The other day [March] I was passing through his class and I noticed the children were listening, joking and having a much better time. The most recent observation [March] was as if they were different children. He looked relaxed – things were quieter. I sat there with a smile on my face and thought, gosh, this is a really nice class. The high spot of the term for me is seeing David happier and saying he isn't going to resign, he is looking ahead. It has been hard – the hardest term for me too!

'I now see myself in a different way. I always thought I was a good listener but it is no good just listening. You have to move it on and arrive at solutions or at least strategies. Being an induction tutor has made me feel good and has boosted my self-esteem, and I know that I have more to offer. The work has improved my skills in people management, including working with SMT, my time management and my interpersonal skills. The subsequent training I underwent as an induction tutor gave me strategies and made me realise I had skills I hadn't developed until now.'

Commentary

Simon teaches in a large, inner-urban primary school and felt motivated to undertake this work when a senior colleague left. It is interesting to compare Simon's story with Joe's story. Both are motivated, with about six years' teaching experience. Both underwent training for the role. However, there is a clear difference in school culture. In Simon's school, the prevailing culture of the school was not conducive to helping him to do his job. There was no whole-school understanding of the requirements of good practice in induction and, indeed, he had to cope with some negative views from staff who had not been informed about his new responsibility. There was no policy and Simon felt he would just have to make the best of it.

In September, Simon could not have known David would have so many problems. Unlike Clare, David found his new job hard and stressful. So Simon had his work cut out. He felt somewhat alone. His new colleague was struggling, and Simon felt he was letting everyone down. However, when he took a step back and viewed the situation objectively, he and David began to focus upon some priorities that were addressed in small steps. These related especially to classroom management, pupil behaviour, identifying groups and individuals and developing strategies to provide targeted support.

Points to ponder

- **Providing support for a colleague who is in difficulty can be challenging, time-consuming and stressful.**

- **Being successful in one school does not ensure success in another. Each school is unique, in terms of pupils, environment and culture. The CEP, if used with integrity, only provides a commentary on a short period of time and does not lend itself to prediction.**

- **All staff need to be in the picture and understand each other's roles and school procedures, and the reasons for these.**

- **Careful diagnosis through observation and discussion is the first step to progress.**

- **Observing 'superteachers' can shatter the confidence, such as it is, of a newly qualified colleague.**

Story 4

Rajinder (primary)

'It was in my professional development interview with my head that I indicated I had enjoyed the challenge of working with ITT students and saw taking responsibility for the induction of a newly qualified teacher an opportunity for my professional development. The LEA at the time was providing a training opportunity for induction tutors and, with the new regulations coming in, it was agreed someone should make sure the school was up to date. I was excited at the prospect of doing something different and hadn't realised how much was involved. However, I felt it would make me a better mentor. We had two newly qualified teachers and I was to be the induction tutor for one and another colleague had responsibility for the other.

'Following the first day of the LEA training course for induction tutors, I felt confident to write a draft policy for the induction of NQTs. It has gone well and the policy is working for me and Chris. Unfortunately, it is a source of frustration for me that my other senior colleague isn't following the process and 'my' policy has not been made public to staff or governors. So, at present, the staff do not understand the new induction process and are somewhat cynical about the reduced timetable and all those observations and meetings. I had hoped for the opportunity to include all this in a staff meeting but our agendas are set so far ahead, there seems to be little flexibility to address this issue because I have no say in our agenda.

'One thing that frustrates me is the lack of whole-school understanding and the lack of consistency in practice. For example, my senior colleague's NQT hasn't agreed any objectives yet and we are now half way through the year. If the policy had been made public and agreed I think we'd have consistency. Having said that, I do feel that, within my own sphere of influence, Chris and I are both making good progress and the school has been helpful in allowing me time to undertake this work.

'When we first met, Chris and I focused on his Career Entry Profile. On reflection, we glossed over his strengths and perhaps we should have talked about these. In section B, although behaviour management was indicated as an area for development, it is not really an issue in this school. However, what Chris was really concerned about was teaching football, gymnastics and maths to children with special needs. So it was on these immediate concerns that we went straight into some objective-setting.

'For example, allowing a half-day for the professional review meeting and write-up has been very helpful. Chris is an able and willing new teacher. Helping him develop his knowledge and skills in physical education has been successful and he has been able to visit another school where a county specialist in PE teaches and he has begun, as a result, to try out strategies and develop confidence. Teaching football is no longer such a daunting task!

'Being an induction tutor has been great for me. It has made me reflect and challenge my own professional practice. For example, we have agreed a system that has changed my approach. It centred around using classroom helpers in a much more structured way where everyone is much clearer about their role, the purposes of the lessons and recording classroom activities. I doubt if we'd have done this if Chris hadn't found it confusing and questioned it.

'The high point for me, so far, has been Chris saying he felt we are organising and providing well for him. Also, I take some satisfaction from the fact that the SMT have now indicated that my draft policy document is helpful – what a breakthrough!

'Another thing I have noticed is that my work as an induction tutor is making me more confident about the contribution I make in this school. I can see how this work spills over into my other work as a curriculum co-ordinator and a manager. One of the areas of focus of my training as an induction tutor has been in communication and the management of meetings. This has made me realise how badly meetings are managed in our school. Also, I have in the past undertaken classroom observations but I cringe now when I think how I wasn't setting them up properly. I am now much more able to challenge poor practice, especially through the careful management of review conversations following classroom observations. I wouldn't have done that before. I feel I have gained really valuable experience by doing this job. When Chris comes to me with a problem, I feel we can solve it.

'When I look back on the year so far there's a great deal I've learnt and a lot I want to do differently. I now treat classroom observation as a process and have practised successful strategies for preparation, observation and review. Review conversations are challenging and, whilst I am better at structuring these, I shall need to listen more and talk less! I also now feel more strongly the need for Chris to come to review meetings better prepared and want him to take a more proactive role in these meetings.

'I suppose the biggest single management lesson for me has been the importance of consistency of practice across the school and how this won't happen without a strategy that involves clear communication with all in the first instance. This must apply to everything we want to do in school.'

Commentary

Rajinder teaches in a large primary school and describes a situation where one of her own professional development needs related strongly to one of the school's needs, i.e. to provide effective induction for an NQT. The headteacher supported her preparation for the role by sponsoring her attendance at an LEA training course, and also created time for her to undertake review meetings and classroom observation.

However, clearly this was not enough to provide the permitting circumstances for a consistent whole-school approach to effective induction to take place. One induction tutor benefited from the latest training, the other did not. While this is a familiar situation and one that can partly be overcome through the two induction tutors working collaboratively, the wider management implications were ignored.

Rajinder's draft policy was not to be shared or developed, and staff meeting agendas were too inflexible to accommodate briefing the staff and giving status to this aspect of continuing professional development. Some of the outcomes of this were a considerable degree of ignorance, cynicism, a lack of consistent practice and frustration for Rajinder.

In a school with two NQTs, one was receiving a very different experience in terms of process from the other. In spite of this, Rajinder decided to do what she could within her own 'sphere of influence'. She found the CEP to be a good starting point and was able to plan with Chris to work on those areas where he felt less confident.

Rajinder reflects upon some valuable lessons for her own thinking about this work and about management in general, which will doubtless benefit her own practice as her 'sphere of influence' widens.

Points to ponder

- Schools always need to rise to the challenge of consistent practice. That is not to say colleagues working in a vacuum in clone-like fashion. It means consistency in the process of management and living out shared values in the life and work of the school. Effective, well managed meetings can be one way to facilitate this.

- Reflecting on your work in a structured way is valuable in so far as the process can raise confidence as a result of success and inform strategies for individual improvement. Rajinder has clearly highlighted some key lessons for her that are illuminating and augur well for her continuing practice.

Story 5   Gillian (independent special school)

'As a headteacher when I first knew I was going to be acting as induction tutor for Angela, I was already aware this role would bring with it additional responsibilities and, hopefully, professional benefits. Where I was less aware was the detail of what this meant, particularly within the context of an independent special school with a very distinctive philosophy. I had experience of working with student teachers and with other staff, but the induction year was new to me and, when the regulations arrived, I had immediate concerns about the sheer amount of paperwork that may be required.

'I felt that the best way to start the whole process was actually to de-mystify it and, in this respect, the first thing I did for Angela was to ensure that she was well settled into the school and had time to get to grips with planning and teaching for the first two weeks. In some respects I had an advantage here because the first term in school did not count formally towards the induction year, although I called this first term 'pre-induction preparation'. This was because discussions were ongoing with the LEA to establish they were willing to act as the appropriate body for the assessment of the year. This led me to question whether there is, in any event, a case for induction starting later as the first term is focused very much on establishing routines and getting to grips with the teacher role. It's not always the best context for 'strategic' professional development.

'By Christmas it had become very clear to me that Angela was a strong NQT who had settled well into school and was achieving a great deal. The time was now right for her to set professional objectives and to establish an induction programme. I wished to ensure there was a clear relationship between the areas Angela had identified in section B of her Career Entry Profile, the objectives defined in her action plan (section C of the CEP) and the actual professional development programme. In this way I was aware that one of the areas Angela had identified was planning and, within this, there was a need to develop more sharply focused learning outcomes. This was carried through in the framing of an objective in section C of the CEP and was then directly commented on during lesson observations and in the professional review meeting. It strikes me that this sense of cohesiveness in the induction period is important if the year is to hold together as a structured period of professional development.

'This link between the CEP and the actual detail of the actual induction programme was also apparent in the visitations Angela made to other schools. I was particularly keen for her to maintain a link with mainstream schools and, in this respect, I set up a regular opportunity for her to observe in a local primary school. One of the foci of these observations was to develop further Gillian's understanding of how ICT [information communication technology] could be incorporated within the curriculum, particularly within numeracy. This knowledge was then applied in her work at our school where she researched available mathematics software, set targets for children's progress in their use of ICT within mathematics and decided on special equipment related to the needs of the children.

'I understood from colleagues in some other schools that the review meeting and the assessment meetings had sometimes been collapsed into one meeting, but I felt these two meetings have distinctive purposes and should be kept separate with separate agendas. I discussed the agenda for the review meeting with Angela and then wrote this for the meeting. Both she and I wanted it to be very focused and, in this respect, there was a detailed discussion about her objectives for short-term planning and a discussion based on newly written short-term plans, together with an evaluation of the work she had undertaken in relation to ICT in mathematics. The assessment meeting, by contrast, focused on the three areas of the standards and used specific evidence as starting points for a more broadly based discussion. In this way assessment of planning, teaching and class management used a lesson observation as a starting point for a discussion on general progress.

'If I were to make a concluding comment about the experience of being an induction tutor, I would say I have definitely derived professional benefit from the experience to date. In particular, I have found the overall structure to be very useful in helping me to think about the need to formalise observations and to be as precise as possible in these. It's definitely a case of the devil being in the detail. It's easy for observations and feedback to be superficial and unfocused, but the structure of the induction year really helps me to be really precise in these areas. I have found there to be very positive knock-on effects for my work with all staff in appraisal/performance management where, again, I am working to be as effective as possible in my mentoring.'

Commentary

When we met Gillian it struck us that many of the elements of her work as an induction tutor were models of good practice. The setting of professional development objectives at the beginning of the formal period of induction was related to the areas Angela had identified when leaving university. However these were deepened, made more precise and related to the particular context in which she was working. The ensuing action plan provided Angela with every opportunity to take these objectives forward and involved a whole raft of professional development activities that approached the same issue from different perspectives. Observation of ICT in another school was complemented by a very clear expectation of Angela to respond to this agenda in her own teaching. During the assessment meetings, the agenda was made manageable through a process whereby the assessment of standards was explored via a specific piece of evidence, which was then widened to include a range of other considerations. Above all perhaps for Gillian acting as induction tutor, the professional benefits of being involved in the induction year were very explicit. She changed from being a little overwhelmed by the paperwork and formality of what she was being asked to do to a circumstance where she was able to make this manageable and so really capable of focusing on the benefits the role brought to both herself and Angela. In essence, Gillian had mediated the whole experience so it made sense within her particular context.

Points to ponder

- Consider the principle of clarity not quantity in your role as induction tutor. Gillian was very focused in her work and this led to manageable but accurate paperwork.

- What do you think about the notion that the induction year should start formally in term 2, with the first term being a settling-in period?

- Gillian was very clear about the distinct purpose of the professional review and assessment meetings. The assessment meetings are not to assess objectives that have been set as part of the professional review, but are focused on whether the NQT has met the national requirements for induction.

- You may wish to consider how Gillian mediated the national requirements to the very specific context of an independent school. How would you mediate the requirements to your context?

In July 2001, OFSTED published a report, *The Induction of Newly Qualified Teachers*. This report focused on the implementation of DfEE Circular 5/99, which was later replaced with Circular 0052/2000 (to be replaced in turn in the autumn of 2001 with a further update).

The evidence used in the report came from inspection visits to schools, which included the observation of NQTs teaching. The sample size of the inspection was 63 schools in 18 LEAs. This included discussions with 220 NQTs, and a questionnaire sent to 220 NQTs with a 50% response.

Many of the outcomes with regard to the effectiveness of induction arrangements in schools are predictable. For example, the variance of quality within a secondary school, the misuse of the 10% release time and the limited use made of the Career Entry Profile.

With regard to induction tutors, it is interesting to note that HMI have inspected and reported on 'training', a term which is not used in the DfEE Circular 5/99. It could be inferred that there appears to be another agenda promoting the notion of 'training experiences' frequently referring to the 'quality of training', and an 'induction training programme'.

The DfEE (now DfES) circular refers to the notion of planned professional development activities (DfEE 2000 Circular). It is understood that such a programme will be based on individual needs which emerge as the year progresses, as well as on those needs which the school requires to be communicated to and practised by all new staff.

It is our view that high-quality induction may not always be compatible with the notion of training. Of course there are times when all staff require some training, but to raise training as a key element of induction is potentially reductionist and may fail to recognise the high-quality monitoring and support provided by induction tutors.

There is perhaps a danger that the report gives the impression that induction is something done to the NQT and that it appears overly concerned with procedural issues.

The report concludes with the view that the Circular 5/99 is clear and helpful and that 'the great majority of NQTs consider the requirements achieve the objective of providing a bridge from initial teacher training to the first teaching post'.

There are several issues which are indicated as being important for future action, especially those which revolve around assessment, consistency and 'target' setting.

However, we consider above all that the quality of induction depends on the knowledge and skills of induction tutors and on the school's creating the circumstances for them to undertake their work. This principle underpins the whole of this book.

Department for Education and Employment   **Annex B**

NQT Induction assessment form for the:

☑   end of first assessment period.   ☐   end of second assessment period.

- This form should be completed by the Headteacher and sent to the Appropriate Body within ten working days of the relevant assessment meeting.
- Where tick boxes appear, please tick the relevant box(es).

Full name	GILLIAN HARVEY

Date of birth   `0` `3` `0` `6` `1` `9` `7` `0`

DfEE reference number of NQT   ☐☐☐☐☐☐☐☐☐

National Insurance number of NQT   ☐☐☐☐☐☐☐☐

Name of school   CASTLEFIELD PRIMARY SCHOOL

DfEE number of school   ☐☐☐☐   ☐☐☐☐☐

Second period of assessment: Is this the school that reported at the end of the first period? ☐ Yes ☐ No

Name of appropriate body receiving the report

HARTSHIRE L.E.A.

Date of appointment   ☐☐☐☐☐☐

NQT's Specialism   ☐ Key stage ▶ *please specify*   KS1
                    ☐ Age range ▶ *please specify*   3-8
                    ☐ Subject ▶ *please specify*   ENGLISH AND LITERACY

Does the NQT work: ☐ Part-time? ▶ *please state proportion of a week worked* _____
                      ☐ Full-time?

Recommendation: ✓   The above named teacher's progress indicates that he/she will be able to meet the requirements for the satisfactory completion of the induction period.
                       ☐   The above named teacher is not making satisfactory progress towards the requirements for the satisfactory completion of the induction period.

Please indicate the kinds of support and monitoring arrangements that have been in place this term.
                       ✓   Observations of the NQT's teaching and provision of feedback.
                       ✓   Discussions between the NQT and the induction tutor to review progress and set targets
                       ✓   Observations of experienced teachers by the NQT.
                       ✓   An assessment meeting between the NQT and the induction tutor.
                       ☐   **Other** ▶   *please specify* _____

- Under the following headings, please give brief details of:
  - the extent to which the NQT is meeting the induction standards
  - in circumstances where the NQT is not considered to have made satisfactory progress, details of the following should also be given in the relevant sections:
    - areas of weakness;
    - evidence used to inform the judgement;
    - targets for the coming term: and
    - the support which is planned.

    Reference should be made to the specific standards concerned.
- Please continue on a separate sheet if required.

Planning, teaching and class management

Gillian is making progress such that she will be able to meet the induction period requirements by the end of the year. Her planning has focused learning objectives and specific questions are posed so that there is a clear link between assessment and the main purposes of the lesson. Teaching is generally very well paced and structured and Gillian's numeracy hour teaching is particularly impressive with very clear expectations and evidence of individually targeted questions. Throughout the term Gillian has demonstrated an ability to develop and retain relationships with her class based on mutual respect.

Monitoring, assessment, recording, reporting and accountability

Gillian is making progress in this areas such that she will be able to meet the induction period requirements by the end of the year. Her assessment of children's learning are generally acceptable and valid and a particular strength is her assessment in numeracy, where she has become adept at setting individual pupil targets and following them through. Records are comprehensive, but Gillian is now working to ensure that they are as concise as possible. Reporting to parents will be covered next term in the formal sense of a parents' evening, although there is strong evidence of Gillian's ability at reporting informally to parents.

Other professional requirements

Gillian is making progress in this area such that she will be able to meet the induction period requirements by the end of the year. At all times she has achieved an appropriate standard of professionalism in her conduct. In particular she has developed an excellent relationship with the teaching assistant in the classroom and has also utilised parental help effectively.

Comments by the NQT: I have discussed this report with the induction tutor and/or headteacher and:

☐   have no comments to make   ✓   wish to make the following comments.

▼

I am happy with the comments which have been made and I would wish to record my thanks to Julie for all her support during my first term.

School stamp/validation

Signed:

Headteacher
(if different from
Induction Tutor)

Full name (CAPITALS)

Date

NQT

Full name (CAPITALS)

Date

Induction Tutor

Full name (CAPITALS)

Date   Date

Induct1   3

Department for Education and Employment   Annex B

NQT Induction summary statement: End of the third assessment period

- This form should be completed by the Headteacher and sent to the Appropriate Body within ten working days of the relevant assessment meeting.
- Where tick boxes appear, please tick the relevant box(es).

Full name

Date of birth

DfEE reference number of NQT

National Insurance number of NQT

Name of school

DfEE number of school

Second period of assessment: Is this the school that reported at the end of the first period? ☐ Yes ☐ No

Name of appropriate body receiving the report

Date of appointment

NQT's Specialism   ☐ Key stage ▶ *please specify*

                    ☐ Age range ▶ *please specify*

                    ☐ Subject ▶ *please specify*

Does the NQT work: ☐ Part-time? ▶ *please state proportion of a week worked*

                    ☐ Full-time?

Recommendation: **The above named teacher has met the requirements for the satisfactory completion of the induction period.**

Comments by the NQT: I have discussed this report with the induction tutor and/or headteacher and:

☐ have no comments to make   ☐ wish to make the following comments.
                                        ▼

Induct2 ━━━━━━━━━━━━━ 1 ━━━━━━━━━━━━━ Over ▶

School stamp/validation

Signed:

Headteacher
(if different from
Induction Tutor)

Date

Full name (CAPITALS)

NQT

Date

Full name (CAPITALS)

Induction Tutor

Date

Full name (CAPITALS)

Failure to complete the induction period satisfactorily

- This form should be completed by the Headteacher and set to the Appropriate Body within ten working days of the relevant assessment meeting.
- Where tick boxes appear, please tick the relevant box(es).

Full name

Date of birth

DfEE reference number of NQT

National Insurance number of NQT

Name of school

DfEE number of school

Second period of assessment: Is this the school that reported at the end of the first period? ☐ Yes ☐ No

Name of appropriate body receiving the report

Date of appointment

NQT's Specialism ☐ Key stage ▶ *please specify*
☐ Age range ▶ *please specify*
☐ Subject ▶ *please specify*

Does the NQT work: ☐ Part-time? ▶ *please state proportion of a week worked*
☐ Full-time?

Recommendation: **The above named teacher has not met the standards for the satisfactory completion of the induction period.**

- Under the following headings, please give brief details of:
  - the extent to which the NQT is meeting the induction standards
  - in circumstances where the NQT is not considered to have made satisfactory progress, details of the following should also be given in the relevant sections:
    - areas of weakness;
    - evidence used to inform the judgement;
    - targets for the coming term: and
    - the support which is planned.
  - Reference should be made to the specific standards concerned.
- Please continue on a separate sheet if required.

Planning, teaching and class management

Monitoring, assessment, recording, reporting and accountability

Other professional requirements

Comments by the NQT: I have discussed this report with the induction tutor and/or headteacher and:

☐   have no comments to make   ☐   wish to make the following comments.

▼

School stamp/validation

Signed:

Headteacher
(if different from
Induction Tutor)   Date

Full name (CAPITALS)

NQT   Date

Full name (CAPITALS)

Induction Tutor   Date

Full name (CAPITALS)

Induct3   2

References

DeBello, T. (1985) A critical analysis of the achievement and attitude effects of administrative assignments to social studies writing instruction based on identified, Eight-Grade students' learning style preferences for learning alone, with peers, or with teachers, unpublished dissertation, St John's University.

Dewey, J. (1933) *How We Think: A Restatement of the Relation of Reflective Teaching to the Education Process*, Chicago: Henry Regnery.

DfE (1992) *Initial Teacher Training, Secondary Phase*, Circular 9/92, London: DfE.

DfE (1993) *The Initial Training of Primary Teachers*, Circular 14/93, London: DfE.

DfEE (1997) *Teaching: High Status, High Standards*, Circular 10/97, London: DfEE.

DfEE (1998) *Teaching: High Status, High Standards. Requirements for Courses of Initial Teacher Training*, Circular 4/98, London: DfEE.

DfEE (1999) *The Induction Period for Newly Qualified Teachers*, Circular 5/99, London: DfEE.

DfEE (2000a) *Performance Management: Guidance for Governors, Governing Bodies and Headteachers*, London: DfEE.

DfEE (2000b) *Professional Development Support for Teaching and Learning*, Circular 0008/2000, London: DfEE.

DfEE (2000c) *The Induction Period for Newly Qualified Teachers*, Circular 0090/2000, London: DfEE.

DfEE (2001) *Good Value CPD: A Code of Practice for Providers of Professional Development for Teachers*, Circular 0059/2001, London: DfEE.

Egan, G. (1990) *The Skilled Helper*, Pacific Grove, CA: Brookes/Cole.

Everard, K. B. (1986) *Developing Management in Schools*, Oxford: Blackwell.

Fullan, M. G. and Stiegelbauer, S. (1991) *The New Meaning of Educational Change*, London: Cassell.

Glenny, G. and Hickling, E. (1995) A developmental model of partnership between schools and higher education, in Bines, H. and Welting, J. M. (eds.) *Managing Partnerships in Teacher Training and Development*, London: Routledge.

Honey, P. and Mumford, A. (1986) *The Manual of Learning Styles*, Maidenhead: Peter Honey.

Hopkins, D. (1997) Improving the quality of teaching and learning, *Support for Learning*, **12**(4), pp. 162–65.

Hughes, M. (1999) *Closing the Learning Gap*, Stafford: Network Educational Press.

Jenson, E. (1995) *The Learning Brain*, San Diego, CA: Turning Point Publishing.

Kerry, T. and Shelton Mayes, A. (1995) *Issues in Mentoring*, London: Routledge and The Open University.

McNair Report (1944) *Teachers and Youth Leaders*, London: HMSO.

Moran, A., Dallat, J. and Abbott, L. (1999) Supporting newly qualified teachers in post-primary schools in Northern Ireland: the role of the head of department, *Journal of In-Service Education*, **25**(2), p. 225.

Moyles, J., Suschitzy, W. and Chapman, L. (1998) *Teaching Fledglings to Fly?* London: ATL.

OFSTED (2001) *The Induction of Newly Qualified Teachers: Implementation of DfEE Circular 5/99.*

Parsloe, E. (1993) *Coaching, Mentoring and Assessing*, London: Kogan Page.

Phillips, K. and Fraser, T. (1985) *The Management of Interpersonal Skills Training*, Aldershot: Gower.

Sammons, P., Hillman, J. and Mortimore, P. (1995) *Key Characteristics of Effective Schools*, London: Ofsted.

Shipman, M. (1990) *In Search of Learning*, Oxford: Blackwell.

Shipman, V. and Shipman, F. (1983) *Cognitive Styles: Some Conceptual, Methodological and Applied Issues* (ed. E. W. Gordon), Westport, CT: Mediax.

Shtogren, J. A. (1980) *The Structure of Competence – The Theories and Facts about Managing People*, London: Chartwell-Bratt.

Simco, N. (2000) *Succeeding in the Induction Year*, Exeter: Learning Matters.

Stammers, P. (1993) Maintaining that first year dream, *British Journal of Education*, **19**(1), p. 29.

Teacher Training Agency (1999) *Supporting Induction of Newly Qualified Teachers*, London: TTA.

Teacher Training Agency (2001) *Career Entry Profile, Notes of Guidance and Standards.* London: TTA.

Tobias, C. U. (1994) *The Way They Learn*, Colorado Springs, CO: Focus on the Family Publishing.

Trautman, P. (1979) An investigation of the relationship between selected instructional techniques and identified cognitive style, unpublished dissertation, St John's University.

Wlodkowski, R. (1985) *Enhancing Adult Motivation to Learn*, San Francisco, CA: Jossey-Bass.

Yeomans, R. and Sampson, J. (eds.) (1995) *Mentoring in the Primary School*, London: Falmer.

Index